P E R F E C T
vinaigrettes

PERFECT vinaigrettes

APPETIZERS TO DESSERTS

BY LINDA DANNENBERG

Photographs by ZEVA OELBAUM

Stewart, Tabori & Chang
NEW YORK

To Gayle Benderoff and Deborah
Geltman, agents nonpareil, with my
admiration and gratitude for their
help, unflagging support, and skilled
diplomacy through the thick
and thin of creating nine books.

Text copyright ©1999 Linda Dannenberg
Photographs copyright © 1999 Zeva Oelbaum

Project editor: Sandra Gilbert
Designer: Susi Oberhelman
Food stylist: Jennifer Udell

Published by
Stewart, Tabori & Chang
115 West 18th Street, New York, NY 10011

Canadian Distribution:
Canadian Manda Group
One Atlantic Avenue, Suite 105
Toronto, Ontario M6K 3E7 Canada

LIBRARY OF CONGRESS CATALOGING-IN-PUBLICATION DATA

Dannenberg, Linda.
    Perfect vinaigrettes: appetizers to desserts / by Linda
Dannenberg; photographs by Zeva Oelbaum.
    p. cm.
ISBN 1-55670-943-9
1. Salad dressing. 2. Cookery (Vinegar) I. Title.
TX819.S27D36   1999
641.8'14—dc21   99-16263
                       CIP

PRINTED IN CHINA
10   9   8   7   6   5

Stewart, Tabori & Chang is a subsidiary of

LA MARTINIÈRE
GROUPE

Acknowledgments

I would like to express my warmest appreciation to the wonderful cooks—some talented professionals, others dedicated home cooks—for their generous contributions to this book: André Soltner, Emmanuel Joinville, Christian Constant, Sylvia Michel, Grace Leo Andrieu, Ariane Daguin, Marcus Samuelsson, Philippe da Silva, Anne, Paul, and Noni Dannenberg, Anne Néel, Jean-Pierre Court, Pierre Gagnaire, Marc Freidus, Joseph Georges, Peter Ochitwa, and Joël Guillet.

To my husband, Steve, my love and gratitude for tasting and critiquing, always with interest, appetite, and an open mind, countless vinaigrettes, sometimes three or four at a sitting. The vinaigrettes are better because of him.

Finally, I would like to thank my publisher, Leslie Stoker, my editor, Sandy Gilbert, and all the talented staff at Stewart, Tabori & Chang—Michael Gray, Jack Lamblough, and Kim Tyner—for making this book such a pleasure to produce.

Introduction 8

Green Salads 17

Composed Salads 35

Vegetable Appetizers 57

Fish and Shellfish 71

Meat and Poultry 89

Fruit Salads 99

Appendix 108

Index 110

A GREAT VINAIGRETTE IS A simple yet sublime component of countless appetizers, salads, and main course dishes. In its most classically defined form, it is a sauce with an assertively tart edge, prepared from oil and vinegar. But today's vinaigrettes, including many in this book, soar far beyond the boundaries of this basic definition, calling for fruit juices instead of vinegar, cream, pan drippings, even honey instead of oil, in countless variations. But at heart the vinaigrette always remains a tart sauce, with a minor but pronounced acidic element balanced by a bland, heavy, smooth element for body and texture.

Variations of the vinaigrette appear in Italian, Russian, Mediterranean, and Scandinavian cooking, and indeed in Oriental cuisines as well. Tossed with salads, drizzled over warm poached fish, spooned atop hot boiled beef, or glossing a plateful of sliced potatoes, green peppers, and hard-boiled eggs, vinaigrette sauces jazz up the most elemental foods, enhancing everything they touch with a harmonious yin and yang of acidic and lipid elements. In whatever form it takes, the vinaigrette imparts a tangy richness and an intriguing spectrum of flavors to every bite.

A colleague of mine, Stephanie Sedgwick, a food writer with the *Washington Post*, once noted that if you know how to prepare a vinaigrette, then you know how to cook. With a variety of vinaigrette sauces, you will be able to dress a salad or a vegetable appetizer, make a marinade, create a sauce for grilled fish or chicken, and whip up a sauce for a fresh-fruit dessert.

At first glance one of the easiest things to accomplish in the kitchen—just a swirl of oil, vinegar, seasonings, and perhaps some herbs and mustard or other elements—the making of a good basic vinaigrette seems, in fact, to be an elusive art. Fine cooks who are undaunted by the prospect of preparing bread, toiling over a complex main course, or creating a complicated dessert cringe when faced with preparing the humble vinaigrette. Like mastering the fundamentals of a superb roast chicken, a great cup of coffee, or

the perfect dry martini, learning to make a fine, well-balanced vinaigrette requires a bit of trial and error and a basic understanding of the components and how they work in synthesis.

CREATING THE PERFECT VINAIGRETTE

There are no simpler recipes in a cook's repertoire than those for fundamental vinaigrettes. Combine two ingredients—oil and vinegar, crème fraîche and lemon juice, olive oil and lime juice, for example—plus salt and pepper, whisk them together and, voilà, you have your dressing. Nothing could be more straightforward. What you need to know to create a perfect vinaigrette is elementary and pertains to virtually all cooking: the quality of your ingredients is of paramount importance, and proportion, the delicate balance of ingredients, is crucial.

Quality. You will never prepare a great vinaigrette out of cheap, low-grade oils and vinegars. You will need the best oils, for example first–cold pressing, extra-virgin olive oils, or even single-varietal olive oils, and the highest-quality wine, sherry, cider, or Champagne vinegars—as well as high-quality sea salt and fresh peppercorns. A vinaigrette will be as good as the ingredients that go into it.

Proportion. Even with the best ingredients it is still possible to go wrong if the proportions are off. A good vinaigrette is a delicate balancing act, using several ingredients in just the right amounts to create a subtly nuanced whole in which no single ingredient calls attention to itself.

The most dependable ratio for a vinaigrette destined for a green salad is four parts oil to one part vinegar. This is not a hard and fast rule: older French cookbooks advise a ratio of three to one, but this makes an extremely sharp vinaigrette. The proportions will change depending on what other ingredients you add to your vinaigrette—mustard, herbs, capers, minced onion, anchovy paste, gherkins—and what the sauce will be dressing. Salads of starchy ingredients such as potatoes, pasta, lentils, or beans require a higher proportion of vinegar to oil since the starches tend to cut the acidity. With composed salads containing starches, or rich, fatty ingredients such as the duck in the Gascony salad on page 38, the proper proportions would be closer to three parts oil to one part vinegar.

The acidic substance you use will also slightly alter the proportion of oil or cream required. If you're preparing a vinaigrette with orange juice or grapefruit juice, for example, both with acidity levels considerably lower than imported vinegars with a mandated 6 percent acidity (domestic vinegars are usually diluted to a 5 percent acidity), then you would lower the proportion of oil to acidic substance to three, or two, to one. Conversely, if you're using an imported vinegar with 7 percent acidity, you may want to increase the proportion of oil to vinegar to five to one.

Salad Greens. In order for the dressing to cling to and coat the leaves of salad, the leaves must be absolutely dry, all moisture spun out in the salad spinner, or very gently patted dry in a clean towel. A salad made with wet lettuces will quickly become limp, watery, and unpleasant.

To figure out serving portions, a good rule of thumb is a handful of greens per person, or about ¼ pound for two generous servings, ⅓ to ½ pound for four, and so on. I always like to make a little extra salad for seconds. There are all kinds of lettuces available at grocery stores now, each offering a different flavor and personality. There are the sweet, tender lettuces such as Bibb and Boston that call for delicate, subtle dressings. There are crisp, full-bodied lettuces such as romaine, red-leaf, green-leaf, and the bland but crunchy iceberg lettuces that can stand up to stronger dressings. And there are distinctive, slightly bitter lettuces such as arugula, endive, and frisée that do well with assertive dressings spiked with condiments such as mustard or ginger, or enhanced with Roquefort cheese. Finally, there is the colorful, tasty, and adaptable mesclun mix, a combination of greens with a slightly bitter edge that works beautifully as a base for a wide variety of salads, and, although once rare, is widely available these days. The mix in a mesclun assortment can vary, but it usually consists of some or all of the following young lettuces or greens: red romaine, green romaine, red-leaf, baby spinach, green mustard, red mustard, red oak, lolla rosa, red chard, radicchio, mizuma, arugula, tat soi, and frisée.

Dressing the Salad. Two final points to remember when preparing your salads: first, while some salads, like potato salads, coleslaw, or perhaps a carrot salad, when they are set aside for a while, improve, allowing time for the flavors of the dressing to imbue the components of the salad, a green salad must be dressed just before serving, a minute or two ahead at the most. The acid in vinegar or in citrus fruits breaks down food, in this case the cellulose of the greens, rendering them limp and soggy if the wait is too long. Second, do not overdress the salad. It is easy to overwhelm delicate greens with too much dressing. The salad—lettuces, potatoes, pasta—should be thoroughly coated, with no excess dressing pooling in the bottom of the bowl.

VINAIGRETTES FOR EVERY COURSE AND EVERY SEASON

To make a good vinaigrette you need no more information than the first recipe in this book, the Purist's Vinaigrette, calling only for oil, vinegar, salt, and pepper. With just this basic formula you can create quite a variety of vinaigrettes by simply varying the oil and the vinegar—extra-virgin olive, hazelnut, or walnut oil paired with an aged red wine, white wine, tarragon, raspberry, rice wine, or sherry vinegar, and so on. But building on the basics, creating imaginative and flavorful dressings to use throughout the meal, is what makes the subject of vinaigrettes so intriguing and so much fun.

THE VINAIGRETTE PANTRY

If you could have only two ingredients in your vinaigrette pantry (in addition, of course, to fine sea salt and black peppercorns), they would certainly have to be a bottle of good, first–cold pressing extra-virgin olive oil and a bottle of good red wine vinegar. But if you love the idea of vinaigrettes, and want to be prepared to make a wide variety of dressings, you should have a few more bottles of oils and vinegars on your shelves, as well as mustards, condiments, herbs, spices, onions, and refrigerator staples such as lemons, limes, and oranges, olives, shallots, parsley, and eggs. Below are suggestions for products you would want in a fully stocked vinaigrette pantry. See the appendix (page 108) for a list of suppliers who will mail-order products mentioned below.

Oils. The oil in a vinaigrette diffuses the flavor of the vinegar throughout the dressing and gives the dressing its structure or body, and its sensuous "mouth feel." The oils with the richest and most sensuous consistency are olive oils. You should have two and perhaps three different olive oils. Extra-virgin olive oil from the first cold pressing is the highest quality olive oil, with a low .5 percent acidity. (Olive oil is graded according to its level of acidity from its free fatty acids; the lower the acidity, the higher the quality. A cold stone press, the first pressing the whole olives go through, yields small quantities of the best oil. Later pressings are done with a hot press that yields more oil, but of lesser quality.)

Extra-virgin oils can range in color from pale gold to emerald green, depending on the olives used, and from a delicately fruity, round, and mellow flavor, to distinctly sweet and fruity, to bold with a slight peppery edge. The most versatile for vinaigrettes are the delicately flavored gold-hued oils. Very assertively flavored olive oils are not good mixers—they have too much personality. With these bold oils, you would create a vinaigrette with only a bit of red wine vinegar or balsamic vinegar, salt and pepper, and at most a crushed clove of garlic. Two of my own favorite olive oils belong to this group of "individualists." One is a Cultivar Primera, an unusual single-varietal oil made exclusively from 100 percent Tuscan frantoio olives, produced by Piccolo Molino, a 400-year-old mill in the hills of Tuscany. The other, from the same producer, is an old-fashioned, rustic-style oil, Velato Rustico, which is the Beaujolais Nouveau of olive oils, a first-of-the-harvest oil, unfiltered and slightly cloudy with bits of pulp that provide a deep olive flavor.

In addition to a bottle or two of high-quality extra-virgin olive oil, you should keep on hand a lower quality pure refined olive oil. Made from hot pressing the olives, from which the pits have been removed, this oil has a 1.5 to 1.8 percent acidity level, a slightly green cast, and a distinct olive flavor. This oil is good for cooking as well as combining in a vinaigrette with a number of ingredients.

Peanut oil, canola oil, sunflower oil, and vegetable oil are good, light mixers to stock, since all are virtually tasteless and thus make good bases for vinaigrettes composed of several ingredients. They are also good for cooking, particularly peanut oil, which has a high smoking point.

Walnut oil, pressed from roasted walnuts, is a light, clear, delicious oil with a marked meaty walnut flavor. It is excellent as a base for some simple vinaigrettes.

Hazelnut oil is another lovely oil with a bold, roasted nut flavor. Hazelnut oil is also very nice in vinaigrettes prepared with a delicately fruit-flavored or tarragon-flavored vinegar. Both walnut oil and hazelnut oil have a tendency to turn rancid fairly quickly, so they should be purchased in small quantities, kept in a cool spot out of direct light (as should all oils), and used soon.

Vinegars. One of the most ancient of condiments, spoken of in the Bible as well as in Greek and Roman documents, vinegar remains one of the most versatile. There is a vast array of vinegars on the market, but all are derived from a fermented liquid—grape, fruit, honey, or rice wines, malt, or hard cider—which gives each vinegar its distinctive flavor. Supermarket vinegars here in the United States usually have an acidity of 5 percent; most French and Italian vinegars have an acidity of 6 percent, or occasionally 7 percent.

A high-quality red wine vinegar should be the first vinegar on your shelf, the more specialized the better (an aged Bordeaux red wine vinegar from France, for example, or an aged Barolo red wine vinegar from Italy). Next, you will need a white wine vinegar, with its light, astringent, grassy flavor; look for white wine vinegars from Bordeaux or Burgundy.

Also on the shelf should be a good balsamic vinegar, made only in Modena, Italy, from unfermented Trebbiano grapes, then aged in wooden barrels of chestnut, oak, cherry, or juniper, from which it takes its dark color and warm, deep, complex flavors. The best balsamics are aged from 8 to 20 years (some, virtually priceless, 100 years) and can cost up to $50 an ounce. There is fraud in the realm of balsamic vinegars, with phony, caramelized, and otherwise doctored vinegars pretending to be true balsamics, so be sure you buy the vinegar of a reputable producer, or at least from a reputable source, such as a good Italian gourmet shop, where they try many samples, know the producers, and choose only the best. Avoid supermarket varieties. A new entry into the balsamic vinegar market is white balsamic vinegar, lighter, milder, and sweeter than traditional varieties, still made from Trebbiano grapes but not aged at all. If you find it, use it as you would a flavored white wine vinegar.

Sherry vinegar from Spain, a vinegar with a beautiful dark amber color, adds a wonderful, nutty, woody, and slightly sweet flavor to a vinaigrette. The best varieties, made in Jerez, are aged in oak casks like the finest sherry.

Apple cider vinegar, made from hard cider, is one of the most economical. It has a nice, tart, apple flavor that is perfect in dressings for coleslaw, fruit salads, and some cream-based recipes from Normandy, France's premier apple-growing province. The most flavorful cider vinegars I've found locally are the organic varieties sold in health-food shops.

Rice wine vinegar from Japan, essential to the preparation of sushi, is a bright, light vinegar without too much personality. It comes both plain and seasoned with salt and sugar. For dieters, the seasoned variety, a bit milder than the plain, can be used on its own as dressing for a salad.

Flavored vinegars, such as tarragon vinegar or raspberry vinegar, usually made from a white wine vinegar base, are less versatile than red and white wine vinegars, sherry vinegars, and balsamics, but they are just the ticket when you want to add one distinctive flavor to a dressing. They usually have a more pronounced aromatic quality than other vinegars, and thus will please your sense of smell as well as your sense of taste.

Melfor vinegar, recommended by chef André Soltner in the two recipes he offers in this book, is an unusual, light and aromatic Alsatian vinegar delicately flavored with honey and herbs. It has been produced exclusively at the Higy vinegar works in Mulhouse since 1922 from an old family recipe. It is quite mild, with only 3.8 percent acidity. Since French law mandates an acidity of 6 percent for vinegars, Melfor is labeled a "condiment" rather than a vinegar.

Mustards. The most frequently used mustard in the preparation of classic vinaigrettes is an authentic Dijon mustard from France, a condiment produced in the Burgundian town of Dijon since the 14th century. Made from black or yellow mustard seeds with the hull removed, classic Dijon mustards are strong, pungent, and creamy, with a pale golden yellow hue.

Moutarde à l'Ancienne, or old-fashioned style mustard, is grainy and brown-speckled, made from coarsely ground mustard seeds with the hulls left in. This style of mustard, occasionally called for in rustic vinaigrettes, is milder than classic Dijon mustard.

I love all kinds of flavored Dijon mustards, because they are a simple way to infuse a vinaigrette with a variety of tastes. Flavored mustards are also terrific as a condiment accompanying roast or corned beef, cold roast chicken, or baked ham. In addition to the classic Dijon and Ancienne style mustards, I always keep a good array of flavored mustards on hand. At the moment, my shelves are happily laden with Roquefort, tarragon, pink peppercorn, Champagne, and herbes de Provence mustards. Each one makes an appealing vinaigrette.

ADVENTURES IN VINAIGRETTES

With a selection of good oils, vinegars, and mustards, some fine sea salt, and a jar of black peppercorns, you are ready to venture into the world of vinaigrettes. The recipes featured in this book reflect a vast range of perspectives on this humble "tart sauce," from the elemental purist's version to luscious, complex sauces such as Pierre Gagnaire's Exotic Fruited Eggplant Sauce for Poached Prawns (page 72); Raspberry-Orange Vinaigrette with Wild Rice Salad (page 47); Piquant Parsley-Caper Vinaigrette for Grilled, Broiled, or Braised Meats (page 97); and Mad Apples's Oolong Tea Vinaigrette for Watermelon and Roquefort Salad (page 103).

While many recipes come from France, where the vinaigrette was officially declared a sauce in the 19th-century writings of the great chef and pâtissier Antonin Câreme, others are Swedish, Italian, Greek, American, Canadian, Chinese, or Caribbean in inspiration. From plain to fancy, from appetizers to desserts, there are vinaigrettes for every cook and for every meal.

G R E E N

salads

Purist's Vinaigrette

This is the starting point, the most basic vinaigrette of all, just oil, vinegar, salt, and pepper. When the vinaigrette is this simple, you need the very best ingredients, because each will be apparent in the dressing: extra-virgin olive oil, aged wine vinegar, fine sea salt, and freshly ground pepper. This recipe calls for red wine vinegar, but you can vary it with sherry vinegar, Champagne vinegar, or white wine vinegar. You can also substitute hazelnut oil or walnut oil for the olive oil. Another variation: add a crushed clove of garlic to the ingredients in the mixing bowl, then set aside for 15 minutes before whisking. Remove the garlic before dressing the salad. Or simply rub the inside of the salad bowl with a clove of garlic before tossing the salad.

1 tablespoon good aged
red wine vinegar

¼ teaspoon fine sea salt

Freshly ground black
pepper

4 tablespoons extra-virgin
olive oil

In a small bowl combine the vinegar, salt, and several generous turns of pepper, and stir until the salt dissolves. Add the oil and whisk until the ingredients are emulsified. Pour over a salad, toss to coat thoroughly, and serve immediately.

Classic French Vinaigrette

The character of this traditional dressing will change depending on the mustard you use. An assertive, true French Dijon mustard is perfect, but you can also try a flavored mustard—a tarragon Dijon, Champagne Dijon (one of my favorites), or an herbed Dijon. I like to serve this dressing over a salad of red-leaf and Boston lettuces combined with a handful of watercress.

1 tablespoon red wine
   vinegar

⅛ teaspoon fine sea salt

6 to 8 turns freshly ground
   black pepper

4 tablespoons extra-virgin
   olive oil

1 teaspoon Dijon mustard

In a small bowl combine the vinegar, salt, and pepper, and stir until the salt dissolves. Add the oil and mustard and whisk until the ingredients are emulsified. Pour over a salad, toss to coat thoroughly, and serve immediately.

Parsley-Shallot Vinaigrette

This wonderful French country dressing, perfect for a mix of two or three green lettuces, such as Boston or Bibb, was introduced to me by a young French friend named Sylvia Michel, who while visiting several years back volunteered to make this vinaigrette one night before dinner. I was surprised to see a vinaigrette so verdant with parsley and so generously studded with shallots, but it was terrific—and memorable—with our salad of garden-fresh greens, and I've been making it ever since.

2 tablespoons red wine
    vinegar

¼ teaspoon fine sea salt

6 tablespoons olive oil

3 small shallots, minced

½ cup loosely packed
    parsley leaves, finely
    chopped

Freshly ground black
    pepper

In a small bowl combine the vinegar and salt and stir until the salt dissolves. Add the oil, shallots, parsley, and several generous turns of pepper. Whisk until the ingredients are emulsified. Set aside for up to 30 minutes, until ready to use. Whisk again and dress salad just before serving.

André Soltner's Lutèce Vinaigrette

This is the dressing beloved by the legions of diners who flocked to the New York restaurant Lutèce under the direction of legendary chef André Soltner. The recipe is simple but distinctive, with Melfor vinegar (an Alsatian honey-based vinegar; see appendix) or tarragon vinegar, a bit of minced onion, and a few drops of Tabasco sauce to set it apart. Another distinctive touch is the proportion of oils. Soltner, not a particular fan of olive oil, prefers a mix of 90 percent peanut or vegetable oil to just 10 percent olive oil in his vinaigrettes. This dressing can be prepared in advance and chilled. If you make it ahead of time, omit the onion; just before serving add the onion to the mixture, and whisk until blended.

**1 heaping tablespoon
finely chopped onion**

2 teaspoons Dijon mustard

**¼ cup Melfor vinegar
(see appendix) or
tarragon vinegar**

1 teaspoon fine sea salt

**⅛ teaspoon freshly ground
black pepper**

2 drops Tabasco sauce

2 tablespoons olive oil

**⅔ cup peanut oil, or other
light salad oil**

In a small bowl crush the chopped onion to a puree with a fork. Add the mustard, vinegar, 1 tablespoon water, salt, pepper, and Tabasco sauce, and whisk until the ingredients bind. Gradually whisk in the olive oil and the peanut oil until the ingredients are emulsified, then taste and adjust the seasoning. Pour over a salad, toss to coat thoroughly, and serve immediately.

LEMON-CHIVE VINAIGRETTE

This is a lovely, light, piquant dressing for a simple green salad—perhaps Bibb or Boston lettuce—to serve after a rich entrée such as duck or pork.

2 tablespoons freshly
    squeezed lemon juice

Fine sea salt

1 tablespoon sugar

3 tablespoons extra-virgin
    olive oil

3 tablespoons finely
    chopped chives

Freshly ground black
    pepper

In a small bowl combine the lemon juice, a pinch of salt, and the sugar. Whisk until the salt and sugar are dissolved. Add the oil, chives, and 4 or 5 turns of pepper and whisk until the ingredients are emulsified.

Sherry-Ginger Vinaigrette for Arugula Salad

T he fresh, pleasing salads, as well as the warm ambiance of a provincial inn, were among the pleasures of dining at Le 6 Bosquet, the Paris bistro where Emmanuel Joinville, a young chef from Burgundy, presided for several years, before decamping to the greener pastures of Vancouver. Chef Joinville shares this recipe, an unusual dressing for arugula, as well as the two recipes that follow, from his repertoire. Le 6 Bosquet may be gone, but, happily, the recipes for some of the bistro's classic specialties live on, in my kitchen, and now in yours.

2 tablespoons sherry vinegar

1 tablespoon hazelnut oil

4 tablespoons olive oil

2 teaspoons freshly grated ginger

Pinch of fine sea salt

$\frac{1}{8}$ teaspoon freshly ground black pepper

In the bowl of a small food processor or a blender combine all the ingredients and process until the mixture is emulsified. Taste to adjust the seasoning, then pour over arugula, toss to coat thoroughly, and serve immediately.

Grand-Mère's Vinaigrette

Many cooks in France make flavorful vinaigrettes by substituting pan drippings from a roast beef, roast lamb, or roast chicken for some or all of the oil in a vinaigrette. In a variation on that theme, this recipe from Emmanuel Joinville's Burgundian grandmother uses the French concentrated beef-stock base Viandox to add a robust, savory taste to an oil and vinegar dressing for a green salad. Do not add salt, since the beef-stock concentrate has plenty.

6 tablespoons olive oil

2 tablespoons aged red wine vinegar

1 tablespoon liquid or gel beef-stock concentrate, such as Herb-Ox

Freshly ground black pepper

In a small bowl combine all ingredients and whisk until the mixture is emulsified. Pour over a salad, toss to coat thoroughly, and serve immediately.

Emmanuel's
Fleur de Sel–Olive Oil
Dressing with Lamb's Lettuce

For a salad of tender, delicately flavored lamb's lettuce, or mâche, Emmanuel Joinville creates a dressing with no vinegar at all, just fruity, top-of-the-line extra-virgin olive oil, fleur de sel, the crème de la crème of hand-harvested French sea salt, and freshly ground pepper. I love to prepare this with a premium, single-varietal olive oil from Tuscany (see the appendix).

½ pound lamb's lettuce, leaves separated, washed, and patted dry

½ cup top quality extra-virgin olive oil

1 teaspoon fleur de sel

8 to 10 turns freshly ground black pepper

Place the lamb's lettuce in a salad bowl. Drizzle with the oil, then sprinkle with the fleur de sel and pepper. Toss lightly just to coat the lettuce and serve immediately.

Christian Constant's Truffle Vinaigrette

At his alluring new Paris restaurant, Le Violon d'Ingres, two-star chef Christian Constant prepares seasonal salads and fresh-from-the-market vegetables with a variety of light, richly flavored dressings. In most, he uses vinegar with a very light hand. One of my favorites is this truffle vinaigrette, which imbues a salad of tomatoes, endives, or mixed lettuces with the deep, earthy flavor of truffles. Truffle juice, the key ingredient, is available from many gourmet food shops and mail-order sources.

¼ cup plus 1 tablespoon
   truffle juice

⅛ teaspoon fine sea salt

Freshly ground black
   pepper

1 teaspoon sherry vinegar

2 tablespoons walnut oil

½ cup peanut or
   sunflower oil

In a small bowl combine the truffle juice, salt, several turns of pepper, and the vinegar, and stir until the salt dissolves. Add the oils and whisk until the dressing is thoroughly blended. Pour over a salad or vegetables and serve immediately. Store any leftover dressing tightly covered in the refrigerator for up to 4 days.

Calvados Country Vinaigrette

SERVES 4

On assignment one autumn a few years ago in the Calvados *département* of Normandy, a region known for its rich supplies of apples and cream, I often enjoyed a very simple salad of young lettuces topped with a dressing created from the area's thick crème fraîche, a touch of its aromatic cider vinegar, and a sprinkling of chives.

2 tablespoons cider vinegar

¼ teaspoon fine sea salt

Freshly ground black pepper

½ cup crème fraîche

3 tablespoons chopped chives

In a bowl combine the vinegar, salt, and several turns of pepper, and stir until the salt dissolves. Add the crème fraîche and 2 tablespoons of the chives and beat with a whisk until the mixture is smooth and creamy, with a bit of air in it. Chill for at least 1 hour to allow the chive flavor to permeate the cream. Serve on a salad of tender greens, such as Bibb lettuce, and sprinkle with the remaining chives.

CREAMY CUCUMBER-DILL DRESSING

There are commercial preparations of this classic salad dressing available in supermarkets, but they can't compare to the taste of the real thing. Prepare this recipe up to several hours in advance and refrigerate it so that the mixture can thicken and develop the flavors of the onion, celery seed, and dill. The dressing, lighter and less viscous than the bottled variety, is delicious over a salad of mixed greens, or over a variety of composed salads.

1 tablespoon white wine vinegar

1 tablespoon freshly squeezed lemon juice

½ teaspoon fine sea salt

½ teaspoon sugar

Freshly ground black pepper

2 heaping teaspoons finely minced onion

¼ cup peeled, seeded, and chopped Kirby cucumber or young, small cucumber

¼ teaspoon celery seed

1 heaping tablespoon chopped fresh dill

3 tablespoons mayonnaise

½ cup sour cream

In a small bowl combine the vinegar, lemon juice, salt, sugar, several turns of pepper, and the onion, and stir until the salt and sugar are dissolved. Transfer to the bowl of a small food processor and add the cucumber, celery seed, dill, and mayonnaise. Process for a few seconds to combine the ingredients. Add the sour cream and process until the mixture is smooth and creamy. Adjust the seasoning, then refrigerate for at least 1 hour. Stir just before serving, then spoon over individual portions of salad and serve immediately.

Simple Caesar Vinaigrette with Homemade Croutons

SERVES 4

This dressing is delicious served on chopped romaine lettuce, as in a classic Caesar salad, or with a salad of equal parts arugula, radicchio, and endive. You can top the salad with homemade croutons if you wish. Note that when you use anchovies you will probably not need any more salt, since the fish is very salty. If you do not use anchovies, add ¼ teaspoon of salt.

2 teaspoons aged red wine
  vinegar

2 teaspoons freshly
  squeezed lemon juice

5 tablespoons olive oil

2 to 3 anchovy fillets

1 small clove
  garlic, crushed

1 tablespoon chopped
  Italian parsley

½ teaspoon
  Worcestershire sauce

3 drops Tabasco sauce

¼ teaspoon freshly ground
  black pepper

⅔ cup shredded Parmesan
  cheese

1 cup homemade croutons
  (see below)

In the bowl of a small food processor or a blender combine the vinegar, lemon juice, oil, anchovy fillets, garlic, parsley, Worcestershire sauce, Tabasco sauce, pepper, and ⅓ cup of the cheese, and process until the mixture is emulsified, about 20 seconds. Pour over a salad, add the croutons, and toss to coat thoroughly. Top with the remaining cheese and serve immediately.

Homemade Croutons

It's very difficult to find commercially prepared croutons that don't taste artificial, overly spiced, and somewhat stale. But it's so easy to make your own that there's really no need to seek an alternative. The Quick Croutons recipe takes just minutes to prepare. The croutons don't have the dense texture and distinct crunch of the Classic Croutons, but they are good in a pinch. The Classic Croutons, also easy to prepare, are tasty little nuggets made even richer if you use butter instead of the olive oil.

QUICK CROUTONS

Toast 4 slices of white bread until well browned. While still warm, brush both sides very lightly with olive oil, then rub the cut side of a half-clove of garlic over one side of the toasts. Trim off the crusts, and cut the slices into ¾-inch squares. Use the croutons immediately, or set aside, uncovered, at room temperature for 1 to 2 hours.

CLASSIC CROUTONS

Preheat the oven to 150°F. Spread 4 cups of cubed Italian or French bread, crusts removed, on an ungreased baking sheet. Bake on the center rack of the oven for about 45 minutes (the croutons actually dry at this temperature rather than bake). Remove from the oven and set aside.

Heat 2 tablespoons olive oil or butter in a large skillet over medium heat. Add 1 crushed garlic clove and stir into the oil. Add the bread cubes and stir with a spatula to coat them thoroughly with the oil. Drizzle with 1 additional tablespoon oil or melted butter, and stir to coat the bread crumbs thoroughly. Stir in ¼ teaspoon fine sea salt. Cook, stirring and turning the bread cubes often, until they are well browned, 6 to 8 minutes. If the garlic turns brown during cooking, remove and discard it. Use the croutons immediately, or set aside, uncovered, at room temperature for 1 to 2 hours.

CREAMY YOGURT–BLUE CHEESE DRESSING

This is a light, flavorful blue cheese dressing with the tang of yogurt. Here the yogurt, instead of oil, gives the dressing its body. Use it over a tossed salad or drizzled on a crisp wedge of iceberg lettuce.

2 teaspoons white wine
  vinegar

¼ teaspoon fine sea salt

Freshly ground black
  pepper

1 generous tablespoon
  minced red onion

½ teaspoon sugar

½ cup crumbled blue
  cheese

½ cup plain low-fat yogurt

In a small bowl combine the vinegar, salt, 6 to 8 turns of pepper, the onion, and sugar, and stir until the salt and sugar dissolve. Transfer the mixture to the bowl of a small food processor. Add the cheese and yogurt and process for 8 to 10 seconds, until the dressing is smooth and creamy. Serve immediately, or refrigerate, covered or in a sealed jar, for several hours before serving.

Tarragon Vinaigrette

When Grace Leo Andrieu, owner of the celebrated Lancaster Hotel in Paris, retreats with her husband and daughter to their country house in the Ile-de-France, she likes to prepare simple fare, including mixed green salads with dressings made with herbs from her garden. This tarragon vinaigrette is one of the family's favorites.

1 tablespoon balsamic vinegar

Pinch of fine sea salt

Freshly ground black pepper

4 tablespoons extra-virgin olive oil

½ teaspoon Maille or other Dijon mustard

⅛ teaspoon Worcestershire sauce

¼ cup loosely packed tarragon leaves, half coarsely chopped, half left whole

In a small bowl combine the vinegar, salt, and pepper, and stir until the salt dissolves. Add the olive oil, mustard, Worcestershire sauce, and the chopped tarragon leaves, and whisk until the ingredients are emulsified. Sprinkle the whole tarragon leaves over a salad, pour in the dressing, and toss to coat thoroughly. Serve immediately.

salads

Coriander-Soy Vinaigrette with Bean Sprout Salad

SERVES 6

This recipe is an adaptation of a salad I loved to order years ago at a small Chinese restaurant off the Boulevard Saint-Germain in Paris. The restaurant is long gone, but the memory of its crisp bean-sprout salads with a variety of toppings lives on. You can substitute julienned chicken or baby shrimp for the ham.

For the vinaigrette

¼ cup rice wine vinegar

¼ cup light soy sauce

2 tablespoons chopped Italian parsley

2 tablespoons chopped fresh coriander

1 tablespoon finely minced garlic

2 tablespoons sesame oil

½ cup peanut oil

For the salad

1¼ pounds fresh bean sprouts, rinsed in cold water and drained

⅓ cup chopped scallions, pale green parts only

¼ pound baked ham, thinly julienned

2 medium eggs, cooked omelet-style, thinly julienned

1 tablespoon chopped Italian parsley

1 tablespoon chopped fresh coriander

To prepare the vinaigrette: Combine all the ingredients in a medium bowl and whisk until the mixture is emulsified.

To prepare the salad: Line the bottom of a deep platter with the bean sprouts. Arrange the scallions, ham, and eggs in three separate sections over the bean sprouts. Sprinkle with the parsley and coriander, then spoon on the dressing. Bring to the table, toss gently to combine the ingredients, and serve immediately. For more informal meals, you can combine all the salad ingredients in a salad bowl, pour in the dressing, toss, and serve.

CREAMY CARAWAY SEED DRESSING FOR COLESLAW

This smooth, rich dressing is ideal for coleslaw, enhancing the shredded cabbage and carrots with the flavors of onion and caraway. It also works well on potato salad. Plan on 6 cups of coleslaw or 3 pounds of small Yukon Gold potatoes (plus ½ cup each of diced red and green bell peppers, if you wish) for 6 to 8 servings. Prepare your salad several hours in advance to allow the slaw or the potatoes time to absorb the flavors of the dressing.

2 tablespoons white wine vinegar or sherry vinegar

¾ teaspoon fine sea salt

2 tablespoons sugar

Freshly ground black pepper

1 heaping teaspoon finely minced onion

1 tablespoon caraway seeds

1 cup mayonnaise

2 tablespoons heavy cream

In a bowl combine the vinegar, salt, sugar, and several generous turns of pepper, and stir until the salt and sugar are dissolved. Stir in the onion and caraway seeds, then add the mayonnaise and cream and whisk until the dressing is airy, thoroughly blended, and smooth. Pour over a coleslaw mixture or boiled quartered potatoes combined with red and green peppers, and gently toss to coat thoroughly. Adjust the seasoning to taste, then refrigerate for several hours; stir once again just before serving.

Ariane Daguin's Dijon-Shallot Vinaigrette with Gascony Duck Salad

D aughter of André Daguin, the renowned and influential French chef from the southwestern town of Auch, long-time New Yorker Ariane Daguin has been bringing the flavors of France to the United States for many years through her company, D'Artagnan. She offers a wonderful assortment of duck and duck products, both prepared and raw, foie gras, cassoulet, and many other specialty items to restaurants and mail-order clients (see the appendix). This recipe makes a luscious and copious main-course salad from Ariane's native Gascony. Serve it with a fresh, crusty loaf of country bread and a hearty red wine from the southwest of France, such as a Madiran or Cahors. Note: If you have a mandoline slicer, use it for the duck prosciutto and the magret.

For the duck salad

- **2 duck confit legs,**
  deboned and sliced
- **½ pound duck gizzard**
  confit, coarsely chopped
- **¾ pound duck prosciutto,**
  sliced paper thin
- **½ pound smoked**
  duck magret, sliced
  paper thin
- **6 handfuls (about**
  ½ pound) mesclun
  salad leaves

For the vinaigrette

- **3 tablespoons red wine**
  vinegar
- **¼ teaspoon fine sea salt**
- **Freshly ground black**
  pepper
- **½ teaspoon finely**
  minced garlic
- **3 tablespoons Dijon**
  mustard
- **½ cup walnut oil or**
  warmed duck fat
- **5 medium shallots,**
  finely minced

Preheat the oven to warm. In a medium skillet set over medium-low heat warm the duck legs until heated through. Transfer to an ovenproof dish and keep warm in the oven. Repeat with the duck gizzard. (The fat on

the duck legs and the gizzards should be sufficient to warm each without sticking to the pan.)

In a large salad bowl combine the warmed duck with the remaining salad ingredients. Toss lightly to combine; set aside. In a small bowl combine the vinegar and the salt and whisk until the salt is dissolved. Add several turns of pepper, the garlic, mustard, oil, and shallots. Whisk until the mixture is emulsified. Pour the vinaigrette over the duck salad and toss to coat thoroughly. Serve immediately.

BACON AND ONION SAUCE PAYSANNE FOR POTATO OR SPINACH SALAD

This is a delicious warm dressing with the rustic taste characteristic of the French countryside. Some of the rich flavor comes from the bacon fat that is used along with the oil in the dressing. Serve it on a warm salad of tiny Yukon Gold potatoes (boiled, then peeled and halved) to accompany barbecued meats or grilled sausages. Or use the sauce to dress a spinach salad with sliced mushrooms, and top with croutons and crumbled hard-boiled eggs.

½ pound slab bacon, diced; or sliced packaged bacon cut into ½-inch strips

1 medium onion, coarsely chopped

½ teaspoon minced garlic

4 tablespoons red wine vinegar

4 tablespoons olive oil

Freshly ground black pepper

In a large skillet cook the bacon over medium heat, stirring frequently to brown the pieces evenly. When the bacon is just light golden brown, stir in the onion and garlic. Lower the heat to medium-low and cook until the bacon is crisp and medium-brown and the onions are wilted but not brown, about 4 minutes. Transfer the bacon mixture to a bowl, then pour off all but 2 tablespoons of the bacon fat from the pan. Return the pan to the heat, add the vinegar, and stir to deglaze the pan, using a spatula to scrape up the browned bits. Add the oil, stir briskly to combine, then remove from the heat, season to taste with pepper, and pour into the bowl with the bacon mixture. Whisk the dressing to combine thoroughly. Pour over potatoes or a salad, gently stir or toss to coat thoroughly, and serve immediately.

ANCHOVY VINAIGRETTE

J ust a couple of canned anchovy fillets add great depth of flavor to a simple dressing. Use this sauce on a tossed salad of mixed greens topped with chopped hard-boiled eggs, which have a particular affinity for anchovies.

1 tablespoon freshly
  squeezed lemon juice

2 teaspoons white wine
  vinegar

¼ teaspoon freshly
  ground black pepper

2 canned anchovy fillets

5 tablespoons extra-virgin
  olive oil

2 tablespoons mayonnaise

In a small bowl combine the lemon juice, vinegar, and pepper, and stir to combine. Transfer to the bowl of a small food processor. Add the anchovy fillets, olive oil, and mayonnaise, and process for 6 to 8 seconds, until the anchovies are pulverized and the mixture is thoroughly blended. Pour over a salad, toss to coat thoroughly, then divide among individual serving bowls, sprinkle with chopped hard-boiled eggs, and serve immediately.

Thyme Vinaigrette with Potato, Green Bean, and Olive Salad

This colorful salad with a wonderfully flavorful vinaigrette is one of my summertime favorites. I prepare it to accompany a barbecue or to take along on a picnic. Since the potatoes, green beans, and kalamata olives have staying power, you can prepare this several hours ahead, or even the night before, and refrigerate until ready to serve.

For the vinaigrette

2 tablespoons white wine vinegar

3 tablespoons lemon juice

3 tablespoons dry white vermouth, such as Noilly Prat

½ teaspoon fine sea salt

½ cup extra-virgin olive oil

1 tablespoon Dijon mustard

¼ teaspoon freshly ground black pepper

1 tablespoon chopped fresh thyme leaves

½ medium red onion, thinly julienned

½ cup chopped Italian parsley

For the salad

2½ pounds tiny new potatoes, unpeeled

1 pound young, thin green beans, trimmed and cut into thirds

¾ cup kalamata olives, pitted and halved

Fine sea salt

Freshly ground black pepper

To prepare the vinaigrette: In a small bowl combine the vinegar, lemon juice, vermouth, and salt, and stir until the salt dissolves. Add the remaining ingredients and whisk until the mixture is emulsified.

To prepare the salad: In a saucepan boil the potatoes for about 20 minutes, until tender when pierced with a knife; drain, cool, and cut into quarters. Boil the green beans for about 4 minutes, until crisp-tender; drain and cool.

In a large mixing bowl combine the potatoes, green beans, and olives. Whisk the dressing again, then pour the vinaigrette over the salad and stir gently with a large spoon until the ingredients are thoroughly coated. Add salt and pepper to taste, transfer to a salad bowl or platter, and serve.

Marcus Samuelsson's Sherry Vinaigrette with Swedish Potato Salad

One of the pleasures of dining at New York's Aquavit restaurant is Swedish chef Marcus Samuelsson's light and tangy caper and dill potato salad. The salad stores well and remains delicious the day after you make it, so it's a recipe that can be prepared in advance and refrigerated. Serve as an appetizer with gravlax, smoked salmon, or other smoked fish, or as an accompaniment to grilled weisswurst (veal sausages) or grilled salmon.

For the potatoes

2½ pounds new or finger-ling potatoes, unpeeled, cut into 1-inch cubes

½ teaspoon fine sea salt

For the dressing

¼ cup freshly squeezed lemon juice

2 shallots, chopped

2 cloves garlic, peeled and crushed

1 tablespoon sherry vinegar

½ cup chicken stock

3 tablespoons olive oil

¼ tablespoon capers

2 tablespoons chopped fresh dill

¼ teaspoon freshly ground black pepper

To prepare the potatoes: Place the potatoes in a large saucepan and cover with cold water. Add the salt and bring to a boil over high heat. Lower the heat to medium-high and boil for about 10 minutes, until the potatoes are soft. Drain, transfer to a large bowl, then set aside to cool.

To prepare the vinaigrette: In a small saucepan combine all the ingredients and warm over low heat, stirring occasionally, for 5 minutes. Set aside to cool to room temperature.

Pour the vinaigrette over the potatoes and stir gently with a large spoon until the potatoes are thoroughly coated. Set aside at room temperature for at least 1 hour to allow the flavors to develop, then stir again and serve.

Kiwi Vinaigrette with Duck, Apple, and Beet Salad

Appetizer: **SERVES 6**
Main Course: **SERVES 4**

This imaginative, colorful, and succulent recipe, for a sumptuous dinner appetizer or elegant main-course luncheon salad, was created by Philippe da Silva, the celebrated two-star chef of the Paris restaurant Chiberta, who recently left to open a romantic inn set in the hills of Provence, Les Gorges de Pennafort. The apples, beets, and endives, dressed with the kiwi vinaigrette, also make a satisfying salad on their own, without the duck.

For the vinaigrette

¼ pound ripe kiwi fruit, peeled and sliced

2 tablespoons Meaux mustard (grainy old-fashioned prepared mustard)

2 tablespoons freshly squeezed lemon juice

6 tablespoons olive oil

6 tablespoons peanut oil

Fine sea salt

Freshly ground black pepper

For the salad

3 medium heads Belgian endive, hard core removed, cut into ½-inch slices

½ pound cooked beets, cut in sticks like thin French fries

1 large Granny Smith apple, peeled, cored, and finely julienned

5 duck confit thighs

½ pound duck gizzards, coarsely chopped

½ pound Boston or Bibb lettuce leaves, left whole

To prepare the vinaigrette: In a blender or small food processor combine the kiwi fruit, mustard, and lemon juice. Process until blended, about 10 seconds. While the blender or food processor is running, slowly pour in the olive oil, then the peanut oil, and process until the mixture is emulsified, about 20 seconds. Add salt and pepper to taste, then cover and refrigerate.

To prepare the salad: In a mixing bowl combine the endive, beets, and apple. Add about ⅓ of the vinaigrette and toss lightly to combine; set aside. In a medium skillet over medium heat warm the duck thighs and gizzards, stirring often, until they are heated through, about 5 minutes. Cut the meat off the bones and slice it into thin julienne strips. In a bowl combine the meat, gizzards, and another ⅓ of the vinaigrette and toss to combine; set aside.

Arrange the lettuce leaves around the edge of a round serving platter. Inside this circle of lettuce, but overlapping the leaves by about ⅓, arrange a ring of the apple and beet mixture. Fill the center with the duck mixture, drizzle the platter with the remaining vinaigrette, and serve.

Raspberry-Orange Vinaigrette with Wild Rice Salad

SERVES 10 TO 12

This is a sweet-and-sour vinaigrette, fragrant with the scent of raspberries and heady with a generous dose of orange-flavored liqueur. I created it one Christmas weekend to dress a succulent wild rice salad studded with bright dried fruits. (If children are going to partake of this salad, you can substitute a mixture of orange juice and apricot nectar for the liqueur.) Colorful and elegant, this salad is wonderful at holiday time as a side dish with a baked ham or a roast goose. Begin preparations several hours ahead; assemble the salad, adding the vinaigrette at least two hours before serving, then refrigerate.

For the salad

- 1⅓ cups (about 6 ounces) sun-dried apricots, quartered
- 1½ cups (about 7 ounces) sun-dried peaches, chopped
- 1½ cups (about 9 ounces) dried cranberries
- ¾ cup Curaçao or other orange-flavored liqueur
- 1½ cups wild rice, well rinsed and picked over to remove grit
- 6¾ cups chicken broth

- Fine sea salt
- 2 cups long-grain white rice
- ½ cup loosely packed fresh chervil leaves, coarsely chopped

For the vinaigrette

- ⅓ cup raspberry vinegar
- ½ teaspoon sea salt
- ½ cup canola oil or other light vegetable oil
- 1 heaping tablespoon Dijon mustard
- Freshly ground pepper
- ½ cup fresh raspberries

To prepare the salad: In a medium bowl combine the apricots, peaches, cranberries, and Curaçao, and stir with a wooden spoon to coat the fruits with the liqueur. Cover with plastic wrap and set aside to macerate for at least 2 hours, stirring the mixture from time to time. In a large saucepan combine the wild rice, 3¾ cups of the broth, and a generous pinch of salt. Bring to a boil over medium-high heat, cover, and reduce the heat to low. Cook for 45 to 55 minutes (the cooking time for wild rice is always a bit unpredictable), until all the liquid is absorbed and most of the grains have cracked open to reveal the white interior. Set the pot aside, covered, to cool.

Meanwhile, in a large saucepan combine the long-grain white rice, the remaining broth, and a generous pinch of salt. Bring to a boil over medium-high heat, cover, and reduce the heat to low. Cook for 15 to 17 minutes, until all the liquid is absorbed. Set the pot aside, covered, to cool.

Drain the fruits in a fine strainer set over a small mixing bowl, pressing the fruits with the back of a wooden spoon to extract all the Curaçao; reserve the liquid for the vinaigrette. In a large glass or ceramic salad bowl combine the two rices, the fruits, and the chervil; set aside.

To prepare the vinaigrette: To the reserved Curaçao add the vinegar and sea salt and stir until the salt dissolves. Add the oil, mustard, and several turns of pepper, and whisk until the ingredients are emulsified. In a small bowl crush the raspberries with a fork. Add the raspberries to the vinaigrette mixture and stir gently to combine.

Pour the vinaigrette over the rice salad and toss to combine thoroughly. Add more salt and pepper to taste, and toss. Cover lightly with plastic wrap and refrigerate for at least 2 hours; toss once more just before serving. Serve chilled.

VERMONT MAPLE DRESSING

My brother, Paul, his wife, Anne, and daughter, Noni, live in northern Vermont, where they have a large garden to grow their own organic vegetables and many maple trees, which they tap in the spring to produce their own maple syrup. Their well-balanced, delicately sweet-and-sour dressing is delicious on a salad of mixed greens with shredded carrots, sliced Kirby cucumbers, thinly sliced baby radishes, and cherry tomatoes.

2 tablespoons red wine vinegar or cider vinegar

¼ teaspoon fine sea salt

1 teaspoon freshly squeezed lemon juice

1 small clove garlic, minced

Freshly ground black pepper

2 tablespoons maple syrup

1 tablespoon ketchup (optional)

6 tablespoons olive oil

In a small bowl combine the vinegar, salt, lemon juice, garlic, and several turns of pepper, and stir until the salt is dissolved. Add the maple syrup and ketchup and whisk to blend thoroughly. Add the olive oil and whisk until the ingredients are emulsified. Pour over a salad and toss to coat thoroughly, or spoon over individual servings of salad, and serve immediately.

Avocado-Herb Dressing

This thick and creamy green dressing, speckled with herbs, is very nice atop a colorful tossed salad of greens and an assortment of chopped raw vegetables such as carrots, radishes, cucumber, and celery. With its thick consistency, this dressing can also work well as a dip for crisp raw vegetables. Be sure to choose a ripe avocado.

1 tablespoon red wine vinegar

¼ teaspoon fine sea salt

¼ teaspoon freshly ground black pepper

1 teaspoon Dijon mustard

4 tablespoons peanut or canola oil

3 tablespoons chopped fresh aromatic herbs (choose three from: chervil, chives, tarragon, parsley, or celery leaves)

1 ripe avocado, peeled and mashed through a sieve

In a bowl combine the vinegar, salt, and pepper, and stir until the salt dissolves. Whisk in the mustard, then add the oil and whisk to bind the ingredients. Stir in the herbs, add the avocado, and beat until the dressing is thoroughly blended and almost smooth. Even when well-beaten there will still be a bit of texture from the avocado. Spoon over individual servings of salad.

GARLIC-BASIL VINAIGRETTE WITH SALADE NIÇOISE

When preparing a salade niçoise in Nice, purists often put no vinegar at all on the salad, instead rubbing the salad bowl with a clove of garlic and simply drizzling a rich and fruity local extra-virgin olive oil over the vegetables and fish. Ordering the salad in one of the small outdoor bistros around town, you might see anchovies substituted for tuna, cucumbers and green peppers for the green beans, and rice rather than lettuce as a salad base. This version is the way I've often enjoyed the salad in the sidewalk cafes of Paris. For a perfect summer lunch, serve it with a chilled dry rosé wine from Provence and a fougasse bread or other thin, crusty loaf and follow it with a bright strawberry or apricot tart.

For the vinaigrette

1 tablespoon red wine vinegar

¼ teaspoon fine sea salt

6 tablespoons extra-virgin olive oil

1 clove garlic, crushed

Freshly ground black pepper

3 large basil leaves, finely chopped

For the salad

1 head Boston lettuce, leaves separated, washed, and patted dry

2 (6-ounce) cans Italian-style light (not white) tuna, drained

6 medium, firm, vine-ripened tomatoes, cut into eighths

2 cups diced boiled potatoes

½ pound haricots verts (green string beans), trimmed and parboiled about 2 minutes, until crisp-tender

1½ cups frozen or canned baby artichokes, cut in half (if frozen, cook as directed, cool, and drain; if canned, drain, rinse well, and drain again)

6 hard-boiled eggs, quartered

1 small red onion, very thinly sliced

¾ cup black niçoise olives, not pitted

6 sprigs basil

To prepare the vinaigrette: In a small bowl combine the vinegar and salt, and stir until the salt dissolves. Add the remaining ingredients and whisk to combine. Set aside.

To prepare the salad: Line 6 individual salad bowls with the lettuce. Divide the tuna among the bowls, placing it in a mound in the center. Surround the tuna with mounds of tomatoes, potatoes, haricots verts, and artichokes. Place 4 egg quarters on each plate, then scatter the onion and olives over the salads. Whisk the vinaigrette again, remove and discard the garlic, and drizzle the vinaigrette over the salads. Garnish with the basil and serve immediately.

Lemon Vinaigrette with Shredded Carrot and Raisin Salad

T he charcuteries of Paris—the original "take-out" shops dating back about 400 years and featuring all manner of cold cuts and sausages, as well as salads and prepared entrées—offer a dizzying array of choices for the hungry shopper stopping by to pick up a few items for dinner at home. One of the most ubiquitous and popular items in virtually every charcuterie, and something I find irresistible, is the shredded carrot salad, sometimes made with raisins, sometimes without. The dressing is light and lemony, with just a touch of mustard for a little zing. Prepare this salad a couple of hours ahead and then refrigerate it so that the raisins can plump a bit in the dressing and the carrots will be thoroughly chilled. For a variation, substitute chopped dried figs or dates for the raisins. You can also use this vinaigrette on a salad of tender lettuces, such as Bibb, or over steamed vegetables.

¼ cup freshly squeezed
   lemon juice

1 teaspoon fine sea salt

1 teaspoon sugar

Pinch of white pepper

1 teaspoon Dijon mustard

¾ cup peanut or canola oil

5 cups shredded carrots

¾ cup seedless raisins

In a bowl combine the lemon juice, salt, sugar, and pepper and stir until the salt and sugar are dissolved. Stir in the mustard, then add the oil and whisk until the ingredients are emulsified. Combine the carrots and raisins in a mixing bowl, pour in about half the vinaigrette, and toss to coat thoroughly; cover and refrigerate the remaining vinaigrette to save for another use. Cover the carrot salad with plastic wrap and refrigerate for at least 2 hours. Toss again just before serving.

Lemon-Lime Vinaigrette

This vinaigrette has the light, bright flavor of the islands—both Caribbean and Greek. I make it to dress a salad of cubed artichoke bottoms served over a bed of Boston or Bibb lettuce, but it is also good over a variety of composed salads, especially those containing shellfish.

2 tablespoons freshly squeezed lemon juice

2 tablespoons freshly squeezed lime juice

1 teaspoon minced onion

¼ teaspoon fine sea salt

Freshly ground black pepper

1 teaspoon Dijon mustard

⅔ cup extra-virgin olive oil

1 tablespoon chopped mint

1 tablespoon chopped parsley

In a small bowl combine the lemon juice, lime juice, onion, salt, and several turns of pepper, and stir until the salt is dissolved. Add the mustard, then slowly whisk in the oil, whisking until the mixture is emulsified. Stir in the mint and parsley and serve immediately.

Anne's Sweet-and-Sour Vinaigrette for an Assorted Vegetable Platter

SERVES 4 TO 6

Anne and Fabrice Néel, proprietors of Château Lamothe, an esteemed wine estate in Bordeaux, are almost as renowned for their entertaining and their memorable meals as they are for their Premières-Côtes-de-Bordeaux reds and whites. Anne and her mother, Madame Perroquet, prepare an abundance of fresh vegetables and salads, as well as fresh grilled fish, for weekend guests, often serving the vegetables—grated carrots, chilled slices of steamed zucchini, peeled, seeded cucumbers, chilled slices of steamed fennel, and chilled strips of roasted peppers—on a platter, drizzled with this sweet-and-sour vinaigrette.

2 tablespoons sugar

2 tablespoons white or red wine vinegar

⅛ teaspoon fine sea salt

Freshly ground black pepper

6 tablespoons olive oil or sunflower oil

In a small bowl dissolve the sugar in 2 tablespoons room-temperature water. Add the vinegar, salt, and several turns of pepper and stir until the salt dissolves. Add the oil and whisk until the ingredients are emulsified. Separately toss each of the types of vegetables you are serving in a little bit of the dressing, then arrange them on a platter. Drizzle the remaining dressing over the vegetables and serve immediately.

D'Chez Eux's Lemon–Crème Fraîche Sauce for Sliced Mushrooms

SERVES 4

This rich, tangy dressing, from the Paris bistro D' Chez Eux, was created for a salad of small, sliced white mushrooms. For 4 servings, use 1 pound mushrooms, stems removed and thinly sliced. The dressing can also be served on a salad of tender greens.

Juice of ½ lemon

2 tablespoons Dijon
   mustard

¼ teaspoon salt

¼ teaspoon freshly ground
   white pepper

½ cup crème fraîche

3 tablespoons chopped
   Italian parsley

In a small bowl whisk the lemon juice, mustard, salt, and pepper. Add the crème fraîche and whisk until smooth and thoroughly combined. Pour the sauce over the mushrooms and gently toss to coat thoroughly. Cover lightly with plastic wrap and refrigerate for at least 1 hour. Divide the salad among 4 individual plates, sprinkle with the parsley, and serve.

Parsley-Balsamic Vinaigrette with Sliced Tomatoes

SERVES 6

Great summer tomatoes need only a simple, aromatic vinaigrette to enhance their allure. When you can find vine-ripened tomatoes—or even better, an assortment of succulent, variegated heirloom tomatoes from a farmers' market—alternate slices of red, yellow, and orange tomato around the platter.

For the vinaigrette

1 tablespoon good aged balsamic vinegar

Generous pinch of fine sea salt

Freshly ground black pepper

¼ cup parsley leaves

¼ cup basil leaves

1 tablespoon chopped red onion

1 very small clove garlic, or ½ medium clove garlic

4 tablespoons extra-virgin olive oil

For the salad

4 vine-ripened tomatoes, sliced

2 sprigs parsley

2 sprigs basil

To prepare the vinaigrette: In a small mixing bowl combine the vinegar, salt, and several turns of pepper. Stir, then set aside. In the bowl of a small food processor or blender, combine the parsley, basil, onion, and garlic, and pulse briefly until the mixture is finely minced. (If working by hand, finely mince the ingredients on a cutting board using a sharp knife.) Transfer to the bowl with the vinegar mixture, add the oil, and whisk until the ingredients are emulsified.

To prepare the salad: Arrange the tomatoes on a platter in concentric circles, pour on the vinaigrette, garnish with the parsley and basil sprigs, and serve immediately.

DIONE LUCAS'S ARTICHOKES VINAIGRETTE

Crunchy with bits of pickle, olive, and hard-boiled egg, this is one of the rare vinaigrettes you can actually sink your teeth into. The recipe, created by legendary cooking teacher Dione Lucas as an accompaniment that could stand up to and enhance the distinctive flavor of artichokes, is adapted from Dione Lucas's first cookbook, *The Cordon Bleu Cookbook*, published in 1947. Lucas was then proprietor of the Cordon Bleu Restaurant and Cooking School in New York. Aromatic with herbs, garlic, and onion, and speckled with chopped fresh herbs, the recipe is a classic that is perhaps even more in tune with contemporary cuisine than it was with the cooking of the late 1940s. Both the artichokes and the vinaigrette should be prepared at least an hour ahead of time so the artichokes can cool to room temperature and the vinaigrette can be chilled.

For the vinaigrette

1 teaspoon fine sea salt

½ teaspoon onion salt

1 teaspoon crushed black and white peppercorns

½ teaspoon sugar

½ teaspoon dry mustard

½ teaspoon Worcestershire sauce

1 clove garlic, finely chopped

1 tablespoon finely chopped onion

1 tablespoon each of finely chopped parsley, chives, marjoram, and tarragon

3 green olives, pitted and finely chopped

1 small dill gherkin, finely chopped

4 tablespoons tarragon vinegar

1 cup extra-virgin olive oil

1 hard-boiled egg, finely chopped

For the artichokes

Juice of ½ lemon

1 tablespoon white wine vinegar

4 large artichokes, large outer leaves removed, top ⅓ of remaining leaf tips trimmed, stem trimmed flat

To prepare the vinaigrette: In a mixing bowl combine all the ingredients and whisk until the mixture is emulsified. Adjust the seasoning to taste, then cover with plastic wrap and refrigerate.

To prepare the artichokes: Bring a large pot of acidulated water (with the lemon juice and vinegar) to a boil over high heat. Place the artichokes in the water head down, and cook for 3 minutes, then lower the heat to medium and simmer for about 15 minutes, until a leaf can be pulled off easily. Drain the artichokes, cool slightly, then remove the small center leaves and the hairy choke. Set aside to cool to room temperature.

Divide the artichokes among 4 small serving bowls. Whisk the vinaigrette to rebind, then spoon into the centers of the artichokes, making sure that each portion has its share of olives, pickles, and egg, and serve immediately.

"MIMOSA" DRESSING FOR ASPARAGUS

The French call this vinaigrette "mimosa" because the finely chopped hard-boiled eggs sprinkled on top resemble the tiny clustered yellow blossoms of the mimosa flower prevalent in early spring in the south of France. This dressing is very nice with cold steamed asparagus (about 2½ pounds for 8 servings) or a salad of mixed greens.

2 hard-boiled eggs, finely chopped or briefly processed in a small food processor

1 heaping tablespoon each of minced parsley, chervil, and chives

3 tablespoons white wine vinegar

2 tablespoons Dijon mustard

¼ teaspoon fine sea salt

¼ teaspoon freshly ground black pepper

10 tablespoons light olive oil

Combine the eggs and herbs in a small bowl, mix, and set aside. In another bowl whisk the vinegar, mustard, salt, and pepper. Gradually whisk in the oil until the ingredients are emulsified. Spoon the dressing over steamed or boiled asparagus, cooked until just tender, then sprinkle the crumbled egg mixture over the asparagus tips. Or pour the dressing over a salad and toss lightly; divide salad among individual serving plates, then sprinkle the egg mixture over the greens and serve immediately.

Chèvre-Chervil Vinaigrette for a Steamed Asparagus Platter

SERVES 4 TO 6

Featuring soft, fresh goat cheese and fresh green asparagus, this is a perfect appetizer for a spring luncheon or dinner, using the season's first local asparagus. Use about ⅓ pound of asparagus per person, about 2 pounds for six. The vinaigrette with its chèvre topping is also a delicious dressing for a salad of young mixed greens.

2 tablespoons sherry
  vinegar

2 teaspoons Dijon mustard

⅛ teaspoon fine sea salt

⅛ teaspoon freshly
  ground black pepper

½ cup extra-virgin olive oil

1 teaspoon finely minced
  shallots

2 tablespoons chopped
  fresh chervil

6 ounces fresh chèvre
  (goat cheese), crumbled

In a small bowl combine the vinegar, mustard, salt, and pepper. Add the oil, shallots, and half the chervil and whisk until the ingredients are emulsified. Sprinkle the chèvre over a platter of steamed asparagus, drizzle with some of the vinaigrette, then sprinkle with the remaining tablespoon of chervil. Serve immediately, passing the remaining vinaigrette in a sauceboat.

Lemon-Zest Vinaigrette for Steamed or Grilled Vegetables

SERVES 4

I love this bright, tangy dressing drizzled over steamed broccoli florets or summer vegetables—lengthwise slices of eggplant and zucchini, for example—brushed with olive oil and cooked over the grill.

1 tablespoon freshly
squeezed lemon juice

1 tablespoon grated
lemon zest

1 clove garlic, finely
minced

6 tablespoons extra-virgin
olive oil

1 tablespoon finely
chopped Italian parsley

¼ teaspoon freshly ground
black pepper

Fleur de sel, or coarse
sea salt

In a small mixing bowl combine all the ingredients except the fleur de sel and whisk until the mixture is emulsified. Drizzle the dressing over vegetables, sprinkle with a pinch or two of fleur de sel, and serve immediately.

Lemon-Mint Vinaigrette with Feta Cheese and Cucumbers

SERVES 4

Feta cheese and cucumbers are a harmonious pairing, the sharp, assertive flavor of the feta softened by the cool, delicate flavor of the cucumber. Adding mint and the astringency of lemon to the mix enhances both elements. The lemon-mint dressing also works well on a simple salad of mixed greens.

2 tablespoons freshly squeezed lemon juice

⅛ teaspoon fine sea salt

Freshly ground black pepper

6 tablespoons extra-virgin olive oil

½ cup chopped fresh mint

4 small cucumbers, peeled and thinly sliced

1 cup crumbled feta cheese

4 small sprigs mint

In a small bowl combine the lemon juice, salt, and several generous turns of pepper, and stir until the salt dissolves. Add the oil and chopped mint and whisk until the ingredients are emulsified; set aside. Arrange the cucumber slices in overlapping concentric circles on a small platter, then spoon the cheese over the cucumbers in the center of the platter. Drizzle the vinaigrette over the cucumbers and cheese, garnish with the mint sprigs, and serve.

SHERRY DIJON DRESSING WITH LEEKS VINAIGRETTE

This recipe is a French bistro classic, a simple, satisfying appetizer low in calories but high in flavor.

For the leeks
6 medium leeks

½ teaspoon fine sea salt

2 teaspoons Dijon mustard

4 tablespoons olive oil

2 tablespoons finely chopped Italian parsley

For the vinaigrette
1 tablespoon sherry vinegar

2 tablespoons finely chopped tarragon

¼ teaspoon fine sea salt

¼ teaspoon freshly ground black pepper

4 large Boston or Bibb lettuce leaves

10 cherry tomatoes, halved

To prepare the leeks: Trim off the roots and the outer green leaves of the leeks, then trim the tops so that only the white and pale green portions of the stalk remain. Cut the leeks in half crosswise and rinse in several changes of cold water to remove sandy grit. Tie the leeks in two snug bundles with cotton kitchen twine. Bring a large pot of water and the salt to a boil over high heat. Add the leeks and cook for 7 to 9 minutes, until the leeks are tender when pierced with a tip of a knife. Set the leeks aside to cool in their cooking liquid. Drain, remove the string, and set aside.

To prepare the vinaigrette: In a small bowl combine the vinegar, salt, and pepper, and stir to dissolve the salt. Add the mustard and stir to combine, then add the oil and half the parsley and tarragon, and whisk thoroughly. Adjust the seasoning to taste.

Arrange the lettuce leaves on 4 individual serving plates. Divide the leeks among the plates, setting them over the lettuce, then spoon the vinaigrette over the leeks. Garnish the edge of each plate with the tomatoes, sprinkle with the remaining parsley and tarragon, and serve immediately.

shellfish

Pierre Gagnaire's Fruited Eggplant Sauce for Poached Prawns

At his eponymous three-star Paris restaurant, Pierre Gagnaire prepares this luscious curry-scented sauce to accompany langoustines poached in a broth fragrant with lemon balm. Langoustines, usually sold in the United States as frozen langoustine tails, are often difficult to find, so I make this recipe with prawns, poached and cooled to room temperature. The sauce is also delicious with broiled rock lobster tails or grilled or broiled shrimp.

5 tablespoons olive oil

1 small eggplant, peeled and diced small

1 large, very ripe tomato, peeled, seeded, and diced small

½ Golden Delicious apple, peeled, seeded, and diced small

¼ mango, peeled and diced small

⅓ slightly green banana, diced small

2 teaspoons strong curry powder

½ teaspoon tomato paste

1 cup heavy cream

⅔ cup fruity extra-virgin olive oil

Fine sea salt

Heat 3 tablespoons of the olive oil in a medium skillet over medium heat. Add the eggplant, stir to coat, then cook until lightly browned, about 8 minutes. Remove with a slotted spoon and set aside in a bowl. Heat the remaining 2 tablespoons olive oil in the skillet over medium heat, then add the tomato, apple, mango, and banana, and stir to coat. Cook, stirring frequently, until the ingredients soften and give off their liquid, about 5 minutes. Return the eggplant to the skillet and add the curry powder, tomato paste, and cream, and stir to combine. Lower the heat to medium-low, and cook, stirring frequently, for 10 minutes.

Transfer the mixture to the bowl of a food processor or blender and process for 8 to 10 seconds, until thoroughly blended. Cover the bowl of the food processor and refrigerate for 2 to 3 hours, until mixture is well chilled. Return the bowl to the food processor, add the extra-virgin olive oil, and process until the ingredients are smooth and emulsified. Add salt to taste, pulse once or twice to incorporate, then serve immediately, either in a sauceboat to pass at the table or spooned over chilled or room-temperature langoustine tails or prawns.

Anne's Lemon-Garlic Dressing for Grilled Fish

SERVES 4

When Anne and Fabrice Néel are not in Bordeaux tending the vines or the cellars of their estate, Château Lamothe in the town of Haux, they can most likely be found sailing in the Mediterranean. Meals on their boat center around freshly caught fish grilled on a little barbecue by Fabrice and served with this simple but delicious vinaigrette prepared by Anne.

Juice of 1 lemon

4 cloves garlic, pressed through a garlic press or finely minced

¼ teaspoon fine sea salt

Freshly ground black pepper

6 tablespoons extra-virgin olive oil

In a small bowl combine the lemon juice, garlic, salt, and pepper, and stir until the salt dissolves. Add the olive oil and whisk until the ingredients are emulsified. Serve immediately, drizzled over individual portions of grilled fish or passed at the table.

Aquavit's Honey-Mustard Vinaigrette with Gravlax

I love many dishes served by chef Marcus Samuelsson at his Manhattan restaurant, Aquavit, where the menu and ambiance are proudly Swedish. But none is quite as irresistible to me as his gravlax, the traditional Swedish salmon marinated in salt, sugar, and dill, and served in a variety of ways, including a gravlax club sandwich. As an appetizer, the gravlax is served with a honey-mustard sauce imbued with a distinctive flavor—Samuelsson sometimes adds a tablespoon of espresso, an ingredient that he finds complements the rich taste of the salmon, and which also adds body and depth to the sauce. Prepare the gravlax a day or day and a half in advance.

Aquavit Gravlax

SERVES 8 TO 12

½ cup fine sea salt

1 cup sugar

15 white peppercorns,
  crushed

2 to 3 pounds fresh salmon
  fillets, skin on, deboned

3 bunches fresh dill

Combine the salt, sugar, and peppercorns. Rub a generous handful on both sides of the salmon, then place the fish in a shallow glass or ceramic dish and sprinkle with the remaining salt mixture. Cover with the dill and let stand at room temperature for 6 hours. Cover with plastic wrap and refrigerate for 24 to 36 hours. Slice very thinly before serving.

Honey-Mustard Vinaigrette

SERVES 6

2 tablespoons honey
  mustard

2 tablespoons sugar

¼ teaspoon fine sea salt

2 tablespoons white wine
  vinegar

¾ cup canola oil or other
  vegetable oil

Freshly ground black
  pepper

¼ cup fresh dill, chopped

½ tablespoon espresso
  coffee (optional)

6 sprigs fresh dill

In a small bowl combine the mustard, sugar, salt, and vinegar, and whisk until the sugar and salt are dissolved. Gradually add the oil in a thin stream, whisking constantly until the ingredients are thick and emulsified. Add pepper to taste, the chopped dill, and the espresso, and stir to combine. Prepare individual portions of the sliced gravlax. Serve the vinaigrette alongside the gravlax on each plate, and garnish with a sprig of dill.

CREAMY DILL SAUCE FOR GRAVLAX

In addition to a honey-mustard sauce, its most traditional accompaniment, gravlax (see preceding recipe) also pairs nicely with a creamy dill sauce brightened with a generous dose of fresh lemon juice.

2 tablespoons freshly
   squeezed lemon juice

Fine sea salt

1 tablespoon sugar

1 tablespoon canola oil or
   other light vegetable oil

½ cup crème fraîche

2 tablespoons chopped
   fresh dill

Freshly ground black
   pepper

In a mixing bowl combine the lemon juice, salt, and sugar, and whisk until the salt and sugar are dissolved. Add the oil, crème fraîche, dill, and several turns of pepper. Whisk until the mixture is thick and emulsified. Drizzle a small amount over individual servings of sliced gravlax, then pass the rest at the table.

San Régis Lemon-Blueberry Vinaigrette for Fillet of Sole

SERVES 4

The San Régis Hotel in Paris, one of the city's smallest and most beautiful luxury hotels, has a restaurant so discreet and intimate it feels like a private club. In this unusual recipe from the restaurant, created to top a warm but not hot fillet of sole, tiny blueberries are studded through a vinaigrette that also includes shallots, tomatoes, and basil. The combination enhances the simple sole with lovely color and flavor, notably the pleasing acidic bursts from the tiny, tart berries. Occasionally on the menu, small raspberries replace the blueberries in the vinaigrette. The dressing also marries well with rock lobster tails or langoustine tails.

3 tablespoons freshly squeezed lemon juice

1/8 teaspoon fine sea salt

Freshly ground black pepper

3/4 cup extra-virgin olive oil

2 small shallots, minced

1 medium ripe tomato, peeled, seeded, and diced small

1/4 cup basil leaves, thinly julienned

1/3 cup tiny blueberries

In a small bowl combine the lemon juice, salt, and pepper, and stir until the salt is dissolved. Add the oil and whisk to bind. Add the shallots, tomato, basil, and blueberries, and gently stir to combine without breaking the berries. Serve immediately, spooning over fillets of sole or lobster tails.

BASIL-LIME VINAIGRETTE FOR GRILLED FISH

This lively, bright green vinaigrette brings the distinctive flavors of the Caribbean to simple grilled fish such as red snapper or other white fish fillets. You can also use it as a dressing for a potato salad to accompany a seafood entrée.

½ cup loosely packed basil
   leaves

2 shallots

½ small clove garlic

Juice of 1 lime

2 tablespoons freshly
   squeezed lemon juice

½ cup extra-virgin olive oil

¼ teaspoon fine sea salt

¼ teaspoon freshly ground
   black pepper

In the bowl of a small food processor or a blender combine all the ingredients and process until the mixture is emulsified, about 30 seconds. Serve at the table to spoon over grilled fish.

Philippe da Silva's Strawberry Vinaigrette for Sea Scallop Salad

Innovative chef Philippe da Silva, proprietor of Les Gorges de Pennafort, an inn near the Provençal village of Callas, plans his daily menus around what he finds in local village markets and in the larger Riviera market of Cannes. One afternoon, after returning with plump, briny sea scallops just off the boat and some baskets of fragrant strawberries, he created this appetizer, an unusual marriage between strawberries and shellfish laid upon a bed of lamb's lettuce. The beautiful, deep-pink vinaigrette is lush and intriguing. The fragrance and fruitiness as it first touches your palate makes you think it will be sweet, but then comes the second hit of bracing acidity. The flavor is a perfect foil for the rich, succulent scallops. Da Silva serves his scallops raw, anointed with a bit of olive oil, salt, and pepper before being dressed with the vinaigrette. In this adaptation the scallops pass very briefly under the broiler to just cook through.

For the vinaigrette

3½ ounces (about 4 large) strawberries, hulled and halved

¼ cup raspberries

2 tablespoons walnut oil

2 tablespoons peanut oil

¼ cup olive oil

1 tablespoon raspberry vinegar

Fine sea salt

Freshly ground black pepper

1 tablespoon simple sugar syrup, or 2 tablespoons sugar dissolved in 2 teaspoons water

For the salad

30 sea scallops, each cut into 3 equal slices

5 tablespoons extra-virgin olive oil

¼ teaspoon fine sea salt

½ teaspoon freshly ground black pepper

½ pound lamb's lettuce, leaves separated, washed, and patted dry

To prepare the vinaigrette: In a blender or the bowl of a small food processor combine the strawberries and raspberries. Blend or process to form a puree. Then, while still mixing, add the oils, vinegar, a generous pinch of salt, several turns of pepper, and the sugar syrup. Blend or process to combine. The mixture should be smooth, thick, and unctuous. Add more salt or pepper to taste; set aside.

To prepare the salad: Preheat the broiler. Arrange the scallop slices on a broiler-proof plate, drizzle them with 2 tablespoons olive oil, and sprinkle with a pinch of salt and pepper. Toss the lamb's lettuce with the remaining olive oil. Divide the lettuce among 6 serving plates. Pass the scallops under the broiler until they turn white and are just cooked through, about 1½ minutes. Do not overcook. Arrange the scallop slices in overlapping concentric circles over the lamb's lettuce. (There are 5 scallops per serving, thus 15 slices per plate.) Generously spoon the vinaigrette over each plate so that each scallop slice is dressed. Serve immediately.

Shallot Vinegar for Raw Oysters

SERVES 4

When you order a platter of raw oysters in the brasseries of Paris, they arrive briny and glistening atop a bed of seaweed, usually accompanied by thin slices of dense, dark rye bread, a round porcelain dish of butter, and a little stainless steel dish of shallot vinegar. Some oyster purists shun any addition to their bivalves; others will use only lemon juice. But there are many shellfish aficionados who must have this simple shallot vinegar to complete their oyster experience.

½ cup white wine vinegar

¼ teaspoon fine sea salt

⅛ teaspoon freshly
  ground white pepper

¼ cup minced shallots

In a small bowl combine the vinegar, salt, and pepper, and stir until the salt dissolves. Add the shallots and stir to combine thoroughly. Set aside for at least 1 hour to allow the shallot flavor to permeate the vinegar. Divide among 4 small ramekins or demitasse cups and serve with oysters or other raw shellfish.

WHITE WINE MARINADE FOR SWORDFISH

MAKES ABOUT 1 ½ CUPS

Swordfish, with its dense texture and pronounced flavor, takes beautifully to a white wine marinade laced with lemon juice, garlic, and a touch of tamari or soy sauce. This recipe will marinate one large (about 2 pounds) swordfish steak or four individual ones. The fish can be grilled on the barbecue or broiled. I also use this marinade on cut-up chicken for the barbecue.

1 cup dry white wine

Juice of ½ lemon

2 cloves garlic, crushed

⅓ cup extra-virgin olive oil

1 tablespoon tamari paste
   or traditional soy sauce

10 black peppercorns

Combine all the ingredients in a glass or ceramic mixing bowl and whisk to blend. Place swordfish in a flat glass or ceramic dish with 2- to 3-inch sides. Turn the fish over several times to coat both sides with the marinade. Cover the dish with plastic wrap and refrigerate for at least 30 minutes but no longer than 1 hour (remove from the refrigerator about 30 minutes before cooking). After marinating the fish, the marinade can be boiled for 3 to 4 minutes, then used to baste the fish as it cooks.

Green Peppercorn Dressing for Grilled Fish

SERVES 4

Green peppercorns, the unripe pepper berries usually sold bottled in brine or freeze-dried, are often used to make a creamy sauce for steak. Less common but also delicious is a green peppercorn sauce with lemon juice and olive oil, for fillets of sole, halibut, haddock, or swordfish.

¾ cup dry white wine

2 shallots, finely chopped

1 tablespoon freshly squeezed lemon juice	6 tablespoons extra-virgin olive oil
¼ teaspoon fine sea salt	1 tablespoon plus 1 teaspoon green peppercorns in brine, drained

Combine the wine and shallots in a medium-size skillet over medium heat. Cook until the wine is reduced by half, then lower the heat to medium-low. Stir in the lemon juice and salt; add the oil and whisk to bind the ingredients, then add the peppercorns. Cook for 3 to 4 minutes longer, stirring gently, then remove from the heat. Spoon over individual servings of sautéed or grilled fish fillets and serve immediately.

Black Olive, Herb, and Tomato Vinaigrette for Grilled Sea Bass

This thick and pungent vinaigrette-based accompaniment to sea bass or other grilled white fish is more like a condiment than a sauce. Studded with oil-cured olives and bits of fresh tomato, and accented with garlic, lemon, and basil, it graces a grilled fish entrée with the distinctive flavors of the Mediterranean. Note that some oil-cured olives are salted, others are not, so you may need to add more salt if you use the unsalted variety. Plan to cook 4 6- to 8-ounce sea bass fillets for 4 servings. Put just a dollop of dressing atop each fillet, and serve the rest on the side, as you would a chutney.

2 medium ripe tomatoes, quartered, seeded, and diced small

¼ teaspoon fine sea salt

½ cup oil-cured olives, pitted

½ cup olive oil

2 small cloves garlic, crushed

½ cup fresh basil leaves, finely julienned

Freshly ground black pepper

2 tablespoons freshly squeezed lemon juice

1 tablespoon white wine vinegar

¼ cup extra-virgin olive oil, chilled

In a medium glass or ceramic bowl combine the tomatoes and salt and stir. Transfer the tomatoes to a strainer or colander and place it over the bowl. Set aside for 30 minutes. The salt will extract juices from the tomatoes, making the tomato bits denser and more intensely flavored; the juices will be incorporated into the sauce.

Meanwhile, combine the olives with ¼ cup olive oil in the bowl of a small food processor or a blender. Pulse for about 8 seconds, until the olives are finely minced. Transfer the olive mixture to a mixing bowl and add the remaining ¼ cup olive oil, the garlic, half the basil, and several generous turns of pepper. Add the collected juice of the salted tomatoes, the lemon juice, and vinegar and whisk to combine thoroughly. Add half the tomatoes and stir; adjust the seasoning to taste. Transfer to a saucepan over very low heat and warm slightly.

Remove the garlic from the warmed dressing. Drizzle the chilled oil over each portion of grilled or broiled fish, top with a teaspoonful of the dressing, and spoon a more generous portion on the side. Garnish the edges of each plate with the remaining tomatoes and sprinkle with the remaining basil. Serve the remaining dressing at the table.

RAIFORT HORSERADISH SAUCE FOR COLD SMOKED FISH

SERVES 4 TO 6

Raifort sauce, made with horseradish, lemon juice, and whipped crème fraîche, is a standard sauce in classic French cuisine, used as an accompaniment for cold smoked fish such as salmon or haddock, or with hot or cold roast beef. Some recipes call for a couple of teaspoons of dried bread crumbs to give the sauce more body, but I prefer the simpler, smoother version.

4 tablespoons freshly grated horseradish, or bottled white horse-radish, drained

1 tablespoon freshly squeezed lemon juice

½ teaspoon fine sea salt

⅛ teaspoon freshly ground white pepper

½ cup crème fraîche, whipped to firm peaks

In a small bowl combine the horseradish, lemon juice, salt, and white pepper and stir to combine. Gently fold the mixture into the crème fraîche until thoroughly blended. Serve immediately in a sauceboat, or refrigerate an hour or two until ready to serve.

meat
AND
poultry

Red Wine Marinade
for Grilled Steak

This concentrated, aromatic marinade is designed specifically for grilled beef, such as flank steak or London broil, but is also appropriate for small shell steaks. This recipe makes enough marinade for 2 large London broil or flank steaks or 4 individual shell steaks or New York strips.

1½ cups dry red wine, preferably Cabernet Sauvignon

2 tablespoons red wine vinegar

1 teaspoon salt

1 teaspoon cracked black pepper

2 cloves garlic, crushed

1 tablespoon Dijon mustard

2 tablespoons chopped parsley

1 tablespoon olive oil

In a saucepan over medium heat cook the wine until it is reduced to ⅓ cup. Pour into a small heatproof bowl to cool. Add the remaining ingredients and whisk until the mixture is smooth and thoroughly blended. Place steaks in a deep glass or ceramic dish, then brush the marinade on both sides of the steaks. Cover lightly with waxed paper or plastic wrap and refrigerate for 2 to 3 hours, turning the steaks every hour or so. Bring to room temperature before grilling. After marinating the steaks, the marinade can be boiled for 3 to 4 minutes and then used to baste the meat on the grill.

RED WINE HERB MARINADE FOR LAMB SHISH KEBABS

MAKES ABOUT 4 CUPS

Lamb needs a marinade assertive enough to balance the strong, distinctive flavor of the meat. This wine-based marinade has generous amounts of garlic and herbs as well as red onion, aromatic elements that imbue the meat with intense flavors. The aroma of the kebabs cooking over the grill is truly mouth-watering. This recipe makes enough marinade for 3 pounds of lamb cut into large cubes, to serve 6.

3 cups dry, hearty red wine, such as a young Burgundy or a Côtes du Rhône

½ cup red wine vinegar

2 teaspoons fine sea salt

½ teaspoon black peppercorns

½ cup olive oil

1 medium red onion, chopped

3 bay leaves

4 cloves garlic, crushed

2 tablespoons fresh thyme leaves

2 tablespoons fresh rosemary leaves

Combine all the ingredients in a large glass or ceramic mixing bowl and whisk to blend. Add lamb, stir well with a wooden spoon to coat all the pieces, then cover the bowl with plastic wrap and refrigerate for 4 to 6 hours, stirring the meat every hour or so. Bring to room temperature, then remove the meat from the marinade and arrange on skewers, either alone or alternating with pieces of onion and red and green bell peppers. Grill immediately.

Pierre Gagnaire's
Red Pepper–Raisin Sauce for
Grilled Chicken or Veal

At the helm of Paris's newest three-star restaurant and one of the most inventive chefs of his generation, Pierre Gagnaire is constantly creating dishes and garnishes that astonish his discriminating clientele. In this tantalizing condiment-style sauce, Gagnaire combines a unique array of ingredients, including roasted red pepper, golden raisins, hazelnuts, capers, Chardonnay, and coriander, creating a colorful and lushly textured accompaniment for simply grilled chicken or meat. Note that the red pepper will have to macerate for two days in olive oil, so plan accordingly.

1 medium red bell pepper

½ cup olive oil

1 lemon, peeled and
   thinly sliced

1 tablespoon capers,
   minced

2 medium shallots, minced

¼ cup golden raisins,
   minced

2 tablespoons ground
   hazelnuts

2 tablespoons sherry
   vinegar

2 tablespoons dry white
   wine, preferably
   Chardonnay

¼ teaspoon fine sea salt

Freshly ground black
   pepper

½ cup fresh coriander
   leaves, coarsely
   chopped

½ cup Italian parsley,
   coarsely chopped

½ cup fresh chives,
   coarsely chopped

½ cup lemon balm,
   coarsely chopped
   (optional)

Fleur de sel, or coarse
   sea salt

Preheat the broiler. Place the red pepper in a small broiling pan under the broiler and turn several times to char on all sides. Let the pepper cool slightly, then peel off the skin with a sharp paring knife. Rinse under cold water, pat dry, then finely dice the pepper. In a glass jar combine the

pepper, oil, and lemon. Seal the jar and refrigerate for 48 hours, letting the flavors of the pepper and the lemon permeate the oil.

Remove the jar from the refrigerator and set aside for about 3 hours to return to room temperature. Remove the lemon and discard. In a mixing bowl combine the red pepper mixture, capers, shallots, raisins, hazelnuts, vinegar, wine, salt, and several turns of pepper. Set aside to macerate for 1 hour. Just before serving, add the coriander, parsley, chives, and lemon balm, and stir to combine. Serve in a sauceboat to be passed at the table. With the sauce, pass salt cellars or small ramekins of fleur de sel and freshly ground pepper.

Orange Vinaigrette for Roast Pork or Barbecued Chicken

SERVES 4 TO 6

Luscious with fruit and zesty with a touch of hot sweet mustard, this citrus vinaigrette, served slightly warm, is a perfect foil for a roast loin of pork or a barbecued chicken.

¾ cup peach preserves

½ cup freshly squeezed
  orange juice

1 tablespoon hot sweet
  mustard

2 tablespoons olive oil

1½ teaspoons tamari paste
  or traditional soy sauce

1 small clove garlic,
  crushed

2 teaspoons grated
  orange zest

Heat the peach preserves in a microwave oven or over low heat on the stovetop. Add 2 tablespoons boiling water and stir to combine. Transfer to the bowl of a food processor or blender, then add the orange juice, mustard, oil, tamari paste, and garlic. Process for about 10 seconds, until the mixture is blended. The sauce can be prepared to this point and then chilled in a covered container for several hours or even overnight, until ready to use. Transfer to a small saucepan and warm over very low heat. Just before serving, stir in the orange zest. Serve in a sauceboat to pass at the table.

PIQUANT PARSLEY-CAPER VINAIGRETTE FOR GRILLED, BROILED, OR BRAISED MEATS

SERVES   6

This recipe is inspired by the classic Italian green sauce that is traditionally served to accompany bollito misto, the savory boiled mix of meats and vegetables native to Milan and Italy's Lombardy region. The sauce is also a fine accompaniment to pot roast, roast or stewed chicken, and a combination of boiled potatoes and cabbage.

½ cup loosely packed
   Italian parsley leaves,
   chopped

¼ cup packed watercress
   leaves, chopped

¼ cup rinsed and drained
   capers

⅓ cup olive oil

1 small clove garlic, peeled

1 teaspoon Dijon mustard

2 teaspoons anchovy paste

½ teaspoon freshly ground
   black pepper

⅓ cup sherry vinegar

In the bowl of a food processor combine all the ingredients except the vinegar. Pulse 2 or 3 times to mix the ingredients, then turn the machine on and drizzle the vinegar through the feed tube and process for about 6 seconds, until the ingredients are pureed. Transfer the vinaigrette to a sauceboat and pass at the table.

Charcutier's Vinaigrette for Cold Beef or Pork

This is one of grand chef André Soltner's prized recipes, given to him by a master charcutier, or pork butcher, from Normandy, Jacques de Chanteloup. Soltner served this dressing often at his New York restaurant, Lutèce, to accompany a rustic terrine of pork, another of de Chanteloup's recipes. The recipe works equally well as a sauce for cold pot roast, a cold pot-au-feu, or cold roast of pork.

1½ teaspoons Dijon mustard

¼ teaspoon fine sea salt

Freshly ground black pepper

3 tablespoons Melfor vinegar (see appendix) or tarragon vinegar

⅛ teaspoon sugar

¾ cup plus 2 tablespoons peanut oil

2 tablespoons olive oil

1 hard-boiled egg (cooked 8 minutes in boiling salted water, cooled 8 minutes in cold water), chopped

3 shallots, peeled and chopped

5 French cornichons, chopped

1 tablespoon chopped parsley

In a small bowl combine the mustard, salt, several turns of pepper, the vinegar, sugar, and 1 tablespoon water, and stir until the salt and sugar are dissolved. Slowly whisk in the oil until the mixture is emulsified. Add the egg, shallots, cornichons, and parsley, and stir just to combine. Spoon a little vinaigrette over each serving of cold meat, then pass the rest at the table.

FRUIT salads

PINK GRAPEFRUIT–ROSEMARY SAUCE WITH FRUIT SALAD

SERVES 6

This salad truly evokes the French Riviera in midsummer. Redolent with rosemary and the scent of orange blossoms, the dressing is adapted from a dish I had several years ago at an inn called the Mas du Langoustier at the tip of the magical island of Porquerolles, off the Riviera coast. In this recipe it is honey, rather than oil, that gives the dressing body. You may substitute any orange-fleshed melon for the cantaloupe.

For the sauce

2 pink grapefruit, peeled, sectioned, flesh separated from membranes, and juices reserved (or 1 cup commercially prepared pink grapefruit sections)

3 tablespoons orange-blossom honey or mixed-flower honey

1 sprig fresh rosemary

1 teaspoon cornstarch

For the salad

1 cup strawberries, hulled and halved

2 kiwi fruit, peeled and cut into ¼-inch slices

1 cup cantaloupe balls

1 cup honeydew melon balls

1 cup raspberries

½ cup mint leaves, coarsely chopped

6 sprigs fresh mint

To prepare the sauce: In the bowl of a small food processor or a blender process the grapefruit sections and the reserved juices until they are pureed. In a medium saucepan combine the grapefruit, honey, and rosemary sprig. Bring to a boil, then lower the heat to a simmer. In a small cup combine the cornstarch with 3 tablespoons of the grapefruit mixture, stirring to blend. Pour the mixture back into the saucepan and stir until the sauce is thick, about 2 minutes. Remove the pan from the heat, transfer the sauce to a mixing bowl, and set aside to cool. Remove and discard the rosemary. Cover the sauce and refrigerate until ready to serve.

To prepare the salad: Thirty minutes before serving, combine the fruits and the mint leaves in a large glass salad bowl. Pour the sauce over the fruit and toss gently to combine. Cover lightly with plastic wrap and refrigerate for 30 minutes. Divide among 6 individual serving plates and garnish each with a sprig of mint.

PINK-GRAPEFRUIT DRESSING FOR AVOCADO-CITRUS SALAD

SERVES 4

This dressing was adapted from a salad served at the venerable Paris bistro Au Chien Qui Fume—The Smoking Dog—set in the old Les Halles market district. The vinaigrette dresses a salad of alternating slices of avocado, orange, and grapefruit sections, artistically arranged on a platter surrounding a tomato rosette.

3 tablespoons freshly
squeezed pink
grapefruit juice

1 tablespoon red wine
vinegar

Pinch of fine sea salt

¼ teaspoon freshly ground
black pepper

4 tablespoons olive oil

1 teaspoon Dijon mustard

In a small bowl combine the grapefruit juice, vinegar, salt, and pepper, and stir until the salt dissolves. Add the remaining ingredients and whisk until the mixture is emulsified. Spoon the dressing over a platter of avocados, grapefruit, and orange sections. Serve immediately.

Mad Apples's Oolong Tea Vinaigrette for Watermelon and Roquefort Salad

SERVES 16

Oolong Tea Vinaigrette, the creation of Peter Ochitwa, chef and owner of Toronto's popular Mad Apples's Restaurant, makes a light and lovely dressing for a salad of cubed watermelon and Kirby cucumber slices, in equal portions, and ¼ part crumbled Roquefort (for example, 2 cups watermelon, 2 cups cucumber slices, and ½ cup crumbled Roquefort tossed with ½ cup dressing will make four servings). The tea's smoky taste beautifully complements the flavor of the Roquefort and the sweetness of the watermelon. Ochitwa also prepares this vinaigrette using Earl Grey tea, serving it on a mixed salad of frisée and Bibb lettuce, sliced mushroom caps, julienned carrots, and yellow cherry tomatoes.

1 oolong tea bag

⅓ cup white wine vinegar

2 tablespoons liquid honey

1 teaspoon chopped thyme leaves

1 teaspoon minced shallots

⅛ teaspoon fine sea salt

⅛ teaspoon freshly ground white pepper

1 cup vegetable oil or canola oil

In a very small saucepan combine the tea bag and the vinegar. Bring to a boil over high heat, then lower the heat to medium and continue to boil for 2 minutes. Remove from the heat and set aside, allowing the tea bag to steep in the vinegar until cooled. Remove the tea bag and gently squeeze it into the pot to extract as much vinegar as possible.

Transfer the vinegar to a stainless steel bowl. Add the honey, thyme, shallots, salt, and white pepper, and whisk until blended and smooth. Continuing to whisk, gradually add the oil in a slow, steady stream until blended. The mixture should not emulsify. Place in a jar, cover tightly, and refrigerate for at least 4 hours before serving. Pour on dressing and toss lightly just before serving; use 2 tablespoons per portion. Leftover vinaigrette will keep for up to 2 weeks, refrigerated in a tightly covered jar.

Spice Island Marinade with Sliced Oranges

ometimes the serendipitous appearance of ingredients in one's kitchen sparks the creation of a new recipe. This was the case one recent winter day when my husband arrived home from a trip to the island of Grenada with samplings of the island's famous nutmeg, cloves, and cinnamon. On the same day I received a shipment of beautiful tangelo oranges from my mother in Florida. The next evening I composed this dessert for our family and a couple of visiting friends. I serve the orange slices accompanied by a plate of rich chocolate cookies.

¾ cup freshly squeezed orange juice

¼ cup Curaçao or other orange-flavored liqueur

2 tablespoons freshly squeezed lemon juice

1 teaspoon grated lemon zest

2 tablespoons mixed-flower honey

2 whole cloves

1 small cinnamon stick

⅛ teaspoon freshly grated nutmeg

6 medium oranges, skin and pith cut off, thinly sliced, and seeded

4 small mint sprigs

Combine the orange juice, Curaçao, lemon juice, lemon zest, and honey in a mixing bowl and stir to blend. Stir in the cloves, cinnamon stick, and nutmeg. Place the orange slices in a shallow bowl, then pour the marinade over them. Cover the bowl with plastic wrap and refrigerate for 1 to 3 hours. Remove the cloves and cinnamon stick, then spoon the orange slices and marinade into 4 individual serving dishes. Garnish each with a sprig of mint and serve immediately.

CREAMY ORANGE-SESAME DRESSING FOR FRUIT SALAD

This is a creamy and delicious dressing with the consistency and color of a rich sabayon (zabaglione) sauce and the pleasing crunch of toasted sesame seeds. Use it on a salad of mixed fruit, combining two kinds of melon balls (cantaloupe and cassava, for example), orange sections, seedless green grapes, sliced kiwi fruit, and peeled, cubed Granny Smith apples. Or serve it in a sauceboat with a bowl of strawberries. For a more dietetic recipe, replace the crème fraîche with an equal amount of low-fat yogurt. You can garnish each serving with a sprig of fresh mint or a nasturtium blossom from the garden.

2 tablespoons freshly squeezed orange juice

2 tablespoons Curaçao or other orange liqueur (optional)

⅛ teaspoon fine sea salt

½ teaspoon sugar

1 teaspoon grated orange zest

1 teaspoon grated lemon zest

2 tablespoons orange-blossom or mixed-flower honey

2 tablespoons toasted sesame seeds

½ cup crème fraîche

In a medium mixing bowl combine the orange juice, Curaçao, salt, and sugar, and stir until the salt and sugar are dissolved. Add the orange and lemon zests and the honey and stir to blend. Then add the sesame seeds and the crème fraîche and whisk until the dressing is smooth and creamy. Pour over mixed fruits, toss to combine thoroughly, and serve immediately.

Red Wine–Thyme Dressing for Strawberries

Serving strawberries with red wine as a light dessert is a traditional and tasty way of embellishing the ripe berries in the bistros of Paris, in homes in the south of France, and in Italy. This recipe expands on the classic theme, adding a bit of sugar, orange juice, and fresh thyme to the young, fruity red wine. Start this recipe at least 2 hours before you plan to serve it.

4 cups strawberries, hulled
  and halved

½ cup granulated sugar

¼ cup fresh orange juice

½ teaspoon fresh minced
  thyme

1 cup fruity young
  red wine, such as a
  Beaujolais, Burgundy,
  or Zinfandel

Gently toss the strawberries and the sugar together in a medium bowl. In another bowl combine the orange juice, thyme, and wine. Pour the mixture over the strawberries and stir to combine. Cover with plastic wrap and refrigerate for at least 2 hours. Serve in stemmed glasses or clear glass bowls.

IF YOU GO—

In your travels, you may want to visit some of the restaurants, hotels, inns, and wine estates mentioned in this book. Contact them at the following addresses:

Aquavit
13 West 54th Street
New York, NY 10019
Tel.: 212-307-7311

Au Chien Qui Fume
33 rue du Pont Neuf
75001 Paris, France
Tel.: (011-33) 1-42-36-07-42

Château Lamothe
33550 Haux, France
Tel.: (011-33) 5-57-34-53-00
Fax: (011-33) 5-56-23-23-49

D'Chez Eux
2 avenue Lowendal
75007 Paris, France
Tel.: (011-33) 1-47-05-52-55

Hotel San Régis
12 rue Jean Goujon
75008 Paris, France
Tel.: (011-33) 1-44-95-16-16
Fax: (011-33) 1-45-61-05-48

Le Mas du Langoustier
83400 Ile de Porquerolles, France
Tel.: (011-33) 4-94-58-30-09
Fax: (011-33) 4-94-58-36-02

Les Gorges de Pennafort
83830 Callas, France
Tel.: (011-33) 4-94-76-66-51
Fax: (011-33) 4-94-76-67-23

Le Violon d'Ingres
135 rue Saint-Dominique
75007 Paris, France
Tel.: (011-33) 1-45-55-15-05
Fax: (011-33) 1-45-55-48-42

Mad Apples's Restaurant
Bloor West Village
2197 Bloor Street West
Toronto, Ontario M6S 1N4
Canada
Tel.: 416-761-1971

Pierre Gagnaire
6 rue Balzac
75008 Paris, France
Tel.: (011-33) 1-44-35-18-25
Fax: (011-33) 1-44-35-18-37

Mail-Order Specialty Ingredients and Food Sources

or a wide variety of olive oils, nut oils, vinegars, salts, peppers, olives, olive paste, anchovies, and imported tuna, contact the following companies for information or a catalogue:

Balducci's
424 Avenue of the Americas
New York, NY 10011
Tel.: 800-822-1444 or 212-673-2600

Dean & Deluca
560 Broadway
New York, NY 10012
Tel.: 800-221-7714 or 212-431-1691

Joie de Vivre
P.O. Box 875
Modesto, CA 95353
Tel.: 800-648-8854

Salumeria Italiana
1551 Richmond Street
Boston, MA 02109-1414
Tel.: 800-400-5916
Fax: 617-523-4946

This wonderful Italian grocery store in Boston's North End, about one minute from Paul Revere's house, offers the unusual Melfor honey and herb vinegar from Alsace and an excellent selection of true balsamic vinegars. They also carry a range of olive oils that includes the Piccolo Molino line from Tuscany and a sprightly lemon-and-olive oil product called Agrumato.

or domestic duck and all kinds of duck products—duck confit, duck foie gras, duck prosciutto, smoked duck breasts—as well as guinea hens, capons, game sausages, duck and veal demi-glace, terrines, and pâtés:

D'Artagnan

280 Wilson Avenue
Newark, NJ 07105
Tel.: 800-DARTAGN or
973-344-0565

or a broad range of domestic and imported cheeses, cut to order before shipping:

Ideal Cheese Shop, Ltd.

1205 Second Avenue
New York, NY 10021
Tel.: 800-382-0109 or 212-688-7579

or a selection of fresh, aged, or herbed goat cheeses:

Little Rainbow Chèvre

Box 379 Rodham Road
Hillsdale, NY 12529
Tel.: 518-325-3351

or delicious smoked eastern and western salmon:

Ducktrap River Fish Farm

RFD #2 Box 378
Lincolnville, ME 04849
Tel.: 207-763-3960

or succulent Maine sea scallops, Maine lobsters, excellent seasonal fish, and exclusive lines of custom-smoked Scottish salmon developed for star chefs such as Daniel Boulud of New York's Restaurant Daniel:

Browne Trading Company

260 Commercial Street
Portland, ME 04101
Tel.: 800-944-7848
www.Browne-Trading.com

or top-of-the-line Brittany sea salts, and seasonal French produce such as wild mushrooms, lamb's lettuce, truffles, truffle juice, and more:

Marché aux Delices

120 Imlay Street
Brooklyn, NY 11231
Tel.: 888-547-5471
Fax: 718-858-5288

or truffles, truffle juice, canned foie gras, and caviar:

Urbani Truffles

29-24 40th Avenue
Long Island City, NY 11101
Tel.: 718-392-5050
Fax: 718-392-1704

Kitchenware

or all kinds of kitchen equipment, whisks, mixing bowls, spatulas, cookware, bakeware, and the Japanese mandoline slicer called a Benriner, popular in many professional French kitchens:

Bridge Kitchenware Corporation

214 East 52nd Street
New York, NY 10022
Tel.: 212-688-4220
or 212-838-6746

(Page numbers in italic refer to illustrations.)

Anchovy vinaigrette, 41
Apple, duck, and beet salad with kiwi
 vinaigrette, 45–46
Artichokes vinaigrette, 62–64, *63*
Arugula salad, sherry-ginger vinaigrette
 for, 24
Asparagus:
 chèvre-chervil vinaigrette for, 66, *67*
 "mimosa" dressing for, 65
Avocado:
 citrus salad, pink-grapefruit dressing
  for, 101
 herb dressing, 51

Bacon and onion sauce paysanne, 40
Balsamic-parsley vinaigrette, *60*, 61
Basil:
 garlic vinaigrette, 52–54, *53*
 lime vinaigrette, 79
Bean sprout salad with coriander-soy
 vinaigrette, 36
Beef:
 charcutier's vinaigrette for, 98
 parsley-caper vinaigrette for, *96*, 97
 steak, red wine marinade for, 90
 stock, in grand-mère's vinaigrette, 25
Beet, duck, and apple salad with kiwi
 vinaigrette, 45–46
Blueberry-lemon vinaigrette, 78
Blue cheese—yogurt dressing, 33

Caesar vinaigrette, *30*, 31–32
Calvados country vinaigrette, 28
Caper-parsley vinaigrette, *96*, 97
Caraway seed dressing, creamy, 37
Carrot and raisin salad with lemon
 vinaigrette, 55
Charcutier's vinaigrette, 98
Chèvre-chervil vinaigrette, 66, *67*
Chicken:
 orange vinaigrette for, 95
 parsley-caper vinaigrette for, *96*, 97
 red pepper—raisin sauce for, 92–94, *93*
Chive-lemon vinaigrette, 22, *23*
Citrus-avocado salad, pink-grapefruit
 dressing for, 101
Coleslaw, dressing for, 37
Coriander-soy vinaigrette, 36
Crème fraîche:
 Calvados country vinaigrette, 28
 lemon sauce for mushrooms, 59
 raifort horseradish sauce, 88
Croutons, *30*, 31–32
Cucumber(s):
 dill dressing, creamy, 29
 and feta cheese with lemon-mint
  vinaigrette, 69

Dijon (mustard), 16
 shallot vinaigrette, 38–39
 sherry dressing, 70
Dill:
 cucumber dressing, creamy, 29
 sauce for gravlax, creamy, *76*, 77
Dressings:
 avocado-herb, 51
 caraway seed, creamy, 37
 cucumber-dill, creamy, 29
 fleur de sel—olive oil, 26
 green peppercorn, 85
 lemon-garlic, 73
 maple, Vermont, 50
 "mimosa," 65
 orange-sesame, 105
 pink-grapefruit, 101
 red wine—thyme, *106*, 107
 sherry Dijon, 70
 yogurt—blue cheese, creamy, 33
Dressing the salad, 12
Duck:
 apple, and beet salad with kiwi
  vinaigrette, 45–46
 Gascony, salad with Dijon-shallot
  vinaigrette, 38–39

Eggplant sauce, fruited, 72–73

Feta cheese and cucumbers with
 lemon-mint vinaigrette, 69
Fish and shellfish, 71–88
 basil-lime vinaigrette for, 79
 green peppercorn dressing for, 85
 lemon-garlic dressing for, 73
 raifort horseradish sauce for, 88
Fleur de sel—olive oil dressing, 26
French vinaigrette, classic, 19
Fruited eggplant sauce, 72–73
Fruit salads, 99–107
 orange-sesame dressing for, 105
 pink grapefruit—rosemary sauce with,
  100–101

Garlic:
 basil vinaigrette, 52–54, *53*
 lemon dressing, 73
Ginger-sherry vinaigrette, 24
Grand-mère's vinaigrette, 25
Grapefruit, pink:
 dressing, 101
 rosemary sauce, 100–101
Gravlax:
 creamy dill sauce for, *76*, 77
 honey-mustard vinaigrette with, 74–75
Green bean, potato, and olive salad with
 thyme vinaigrette, *42*, 43

Green peppercorn dressing, 85
Greens, salad, 11

Herb:
avocado dressing, 51
black olive, and tomato vinaigrette, 86,
    87–88
red wine marinade, 91
Honey-mustard vinaigrette, 74–75
Horseradish sauce, raifort, 88

Kiwi vinaigrette, 45–46

Lamb shish kebabs, red wine herb
    marinade for, 91
Lamb's lettuce with fleur de sel—olive
    oil dressing, 26
Leeks vinaigrette, 70
Lemon:
blueberry vinaigrette, 78
chive vinaigrette, 22, *23*
crème fraîche sauce, 59
garlic dressing, 73
lime vinaigrette, 56
mint vinaigrette, 69
vinaigrette, 55
zest vinaigrette, 68
Lime:
basil vinaigrette, 79
lemon vinaigrette, 56

Maple dressing, Vermont, 50
Marinades:
red wine, 90
red wine herb, 91
Spice Island, 104
white wine, 84
"Mimosa" dressing, 65
Mint-lemon vinaigrette, 69
Mushrooms, lemon—crème fraîche
    sauce for, 59
Mustard(s), 16
honey vinaigrette, 74–75
see also Dijon

Niçoise salad with garlic-basil vinai-
    grette, 52–54, *53*

Oils, 10, 13–14
ratio of vinegar to, 10–11
Olive:
black, herb, and tomato vinaigrette,
    86, 87–88
potato, and green bean salad with
    thyme vinaigrette, 42, 43
Olive oil(s), 10, 12, 13
fleur de sel dressing, 26

Onion and bacon sauce paysanne, 40
Oolong tea vinaigrette, *102*, 103
Orange(s):
raspberry vinaigrette, 47–48, *49*
sesame dressing, 105
Spice Island marinade with, 104
vinaigrette, 95
Oysters, shallot vinegar for, 83

Pantry items, 12–16
Parsley:
balsamic vinaigrette, 60, 61
caper vinaigrette, 96, 97
shallot vinaigrette, 20
Pepper, red,—raisin sauce, 92–94, *93*
Peppercorn, green, dressing, 85
Pork:
charcutier's vinaigrette for, 98
orange vinaigrette for, 95
Potato salad:
bacon and onion sauce paysanne for, 40
caraway seed dressing for, 37
green bean, olive and, with thyme
    vinaigrette, 42, *43*
Swedish, sherry vinaigrette with, 44
Prawns, fruited eggplant sauce for, 72–73
Purist's vinaigrette, 18

Raifort horseradish sauce, 88
Raisin:
and carrot salad with lemon
    vinaigrette, 55
red pepper sauce, 92–94, *93*
Raspberry-orange vinaigrette, 47–48, *49*
Roquefort and watermelon salad, oolong
    tea vinaigrette for, *102*, 103
Rosemary—pink grapefruit sauce, 100–101

Sauces:
bacon and onion, paysanne, 40
dill, creamy, *76*, 77
fruited eggplant, 72–73
lemon—crème fraîche, 59
pink grapefruit—rosemary, 100–101
raifort horseradish, 88
red pepper—raisin, 92–94, *93*
Sea bass, black olive, herb, and tomato
    vinaigrette for, *86*, 87–88
Sea scallop salad with strawberry
    vinaigrette, 80–82, *81*
Sesame-orange dressing, creamy, 105
Shallot:
Dijon vinaigrette, 38–39
parsley vinaigrette, 20
vinegar for raw oysters, 83
Sherry:
Dijon dressing, 70

ginger vinaigrette, 24
vinaigrette, 44
Sole, lemon-blueberry vinaigrette for, 78
Soy-coriander vinaigrette, 36
Spice Island marinade, 104
Spinach salad, bacon and onion sauce
    paysanne for, 40
Steak, red wine marinade for, 90
Strawberry(ies):
    red wine—thyme dressing for, *106, 107*
    vinaigrette, 80–82, *81*
Swedish:
    dill sauce, creamy, *76, 77*
    honey-mustard vinaigrette, 74–75
    potato salad with sherry vinaigrette, 44
Sweet-and-sour vinaigrette, 58
Swordfish, marinade for, 84

Tarragon vinaigrette, 34
Tea, oolong, vinaigrette, *102, 103*
Thyme:
    red wine dressing for strawberries,
    106, 107
    vinaigrette, *42, 43*
Tomato(es):
    black olive, and herb vinaigrette,
    86, 87–88
    with parsley-balsamic vinaigrette,
    60, 61
Truffle vinaigrette, 27

Veal, red pepper—raisin
    sauce for, 92–94, *93*
Vegetables, steamed or grilled, lemon-
    zest vinaigrette for, 68
Vermont maple dressing, 50
Vinaigrettes:
    anchovy, 41
    André Soltner's Lutèce, 21
    basil-lime, 79
    black olive, herb, and tomato, *86,* 87–88
    Caesar, simple, *30,* 31–32
    Calvados country, 28
    charcutier's, 98
    chèvre-chervil, *66, 67*

coriander-soy, 36
Dijon-shallot, 38–39
dressing salad with, 12
French, classic, 19
garlic-basil, 52–54, *53*
grand-mère's, 25
honey-mustard, 74–75
kiwi, 45–46
lemon, 55
lemon-blueberry, 78
lemon-chive, 22, *23*
lemon-lime, 56
lemon-mint, 69
lemon-zest, 68
making, 10–11
oolong tea, *102, 103*
orange, 95
pantry items for, 12–16
parsley-balsamic, *60, 61*
parsley-caper, *96, 97*
parsley-shallot, 20
purist's, 18
raspberry-orange, 47–48, *49*
sherry, 44
sherry-ginger, 24
strawberry, 80–82, *81*
sweet-and-sour, 58
tarragon, 34
thyme, *42, 43*
truffle, 27
Vinegar(s), 10, 12, 14–15
    ratio of oil to, 10–11
    shallot, for raw oysters, 83

Watermelon and Roquefort salad,
    oolong tea vinaigrette for, *102, 103*
Wild rice salad with raspberry-orange
    vinaigrette, 47–48, *49*
Wine:
    red, herb marinade, 91
    red, marinade, 90
    red, —thyme dressing, *106, 107*
    white, marinade, 84

Yogurt—blue cheese dressing, 33